YEADON'S REGISTER

of

L N E R

LOCOMOTIVES

Volume Forty-Three Part A

Class J71 & J72

YEADON'S REGISTER OF L.N.E.R. LOCOMOTIVES - VOLUME 43A

EDITORS NOTE AND ACKNOWLEDGEMENTS

Welcome to Volume 43 of *Yeadon's Register of LNER Locomotives* - or to be more precise Part A of Volume 43. Once again the wealth of material was such that we had to spilt the volume into two parts to make it manageable. It seems unlikely that we will ever have to split any of the future volumes into three parts. Once you realise what had to go into this volume - Part B will follow next in line - you will hopefully appreciate why it became necessary for the two separate presentations of the North Eastern 0-6-0 tank classes.

The two largest classes, J71 and J72, share Part A whilst Part B will bring the other classes into line - J73 to J80 and the NER '44' class - to finish off these popular and somewhat long-lived tank engines.

A whole host of people have once again been involved one way or another in the production of this Register and it only remains to thank them for their various contributions. Amongst them are Eric Fry, Mike Lake, Tina Potter. Richard Cook, David Crossland, Andy Crawford and Steve Waddington of Amadeus Press. Judy Burg, Helen & Kate, Jean & Simon. Thanks.

The catalogue references for the locomotives featured in this volume are as follows:
DYE 1/50; DYE 1/104; DYE 2/6; DYE 3/40; DYE 3/74; DYE 3/302.

We would like to pass on our thanks to the following photographic contributors, many of whom, sadly, are no longer with us: I.C.Allen, J.W.Armstrong, R.J.Buckley, H.C.Casserley, G.Coltas, R.C.Copeman, A.B.Crompton, D.A.Dant, C.E.Dixon, A.G.Ellis, N.Fields, A.G.Forsyth, E.V.Fry, P.H.Groom, P.J.Hughes, C.Lawson-Kerr, R.A.Panting, H.Percy, J.Robertson, J.F.Robinson, C.J.B.Sanderson, E.E.Smith, Neville Stead, W.H.Tate, D.L.Wilkinson, P.Wilson, W.B.Yeadon.

The Yeadon Collection is available for inspection and anyone who wishes to inspect it should contact:-
The Archivist
Brynmor Jones Library
University of Hull
Hull
HU6 7RX
Tel: 01482-465265
A catalogue of the Yeadon collection is available.

First published in the United Kingdom by
BOOK LAW PUBLICATIONS 2007 in association with CHALLENGER
382 Carlton Hill, Nottingham, NG4 1JA.
Printed and bound by The Amadeus Press, Cleckheaton, West Yorkshire.

INTRODUCTION

General

For ease of reference, a numerical index for the J71 class has been included on page 102. The index lists the original number, the 1946 number and the page number where the engine history will be found. As a cross reference a secondary table lists the 1946 number with the original number.

J71

All of the one hundred and twenty North Eastern Railway Class E 0-6-0Ts, introduced by Thomas Worsdell in 1886, survived to Grouping to become LNER Class J71. The design was intended to be the standard shunting engine on the NER and that is precisely what it became. The sixty built during Thomas Worsdell's tenure were added to by his brother Wilson between 1890 and 1895, when he became Locomotive Superintendent of the North Eastern. Three years later Wilson introduced his version of the E class, the E1 (see Class J72), which was basically the same but with smaller wheels.

All the J71 were constructed at Darlington, the first four batches consisting of ten in each but these were followed by two lots of twenty each during the period 1890 to 1892. Thereafter four more batches of ten completed the class. The running numbers ranged from 27 to 1864 and took up gaps created by withdrawal of worn out engines. Under the LNER renumbering scheme of 1946 the 87 surviving J71's became 8230 to 8316 in order of building. There were considerable detail differences between the various batches at building, and these ranged from 16in. to 16¾in. cylinder diameter, the shape of the ends of the frames, wheel diameter and even the use of second hand material, including wheels, for one lot of ten. During NER days the cylinder diameter was altered on many of the class, most being rebuilt with 16¾in. size whilst some had 16½in cylinders fitted. Four engines reverted to 16in. diameter cylinders after being built with the larger size. Two engines received 17in cylinders, No.1155 in October 1910, and No.1199 in March 1921. For its special duties at Dunston staiths, No.1688 was fitted with 18in. diameter cylinders in October 1903 and apparently kept them until withdrawn in 1959 although new cylinders had been fitted in 1930 and again in 1952.

The boiler used on Class J71 (LNER Diagram 73) was identical to and completely interchangeable with those used by J72 class, although prior to Grouping the practice was little used. The boiler type was also used to reboiler some older 0-6-0T classes, such as NER '44' and '964A'. Two of these boilers off Class '44' saw further use on classes J71 and J72 after withdrawal of these engines.

Prior to Grouping some 380 Diagram 73 boilers had been built, all by Darlington works except for twenty-five by Armstrong, Whitworth for the 1922 batch (Nos.2313 to 2337) of J72 class made by them. The LNER constructed another 159 of these boilers, ninety by Darlington, fifty-nine by Hawthorn, Leslie and ten at Doncaster for the new J72's built there in 1925. British Railways added another 103 to the total, built at Darlington, of which twenty-eight went into new J72 class engines Nos.69001 to 69028.

This brought the total to 642, built over the years 1886 to 1957. Although all were the same size, there were constructional changes introduced down the years, the main one being the use from November 1936 of a single plate for the barrel in place of three butt-jointed rings. This change did not introduce a separate boiler classification, as was the case with some other NER boilers, nor did it affect the position of the dome.

As recounted above, some Diagram 73 boilers were built elsewhere than at Darlington. These particular boilers carried numbers applied by their makers until June 1934, when Darlington decided to integrate them into their own series (for further elaboration on the Darlington renumbering the reader is referred to the RCTS series *Locomotives of the LNER* Part 10A, page 69). Class J72 Nos.2313 to 2337 had been given boiler numbers E21/1 to E21/25 by Armstrong, Whitworth when built in 1922. These became 51 to 75 in sequence when each visited works from 1934 onwards. During the four years 1928 to 1931 Hawthorn, Leslie constructed three batches of Diagram 73 boilers for use as replacements. Thirty were made in 1928/9 numbered 8085 to 8114, and these were retained (except for 8099, see later). Fifteen more appeared in 1929/30 and these carried numbers 888 to 902 and were renumbered 88 to 102 in sequence from 1934. Finally, in 1931 Hawthorn, Leslie made fourteen more, numbered 4581 to 4594 and these kept their same numbers. Reverting back to the early days of the LNER, the ten new J72's built at Doncaster in 1925 carried that works boiler numbers 7953 to 7962. Again these did not conflict with the Darlington series and were retained.

Over the long lifetime of the J71 class the intended work carried out by the engines was altered in a number of instances and the steam brake, which was all that was required for goods shunting, was changed to both the Westinghouse and the vacuum ejector types for handling carriage stock. The tables reveal which engines were so altered.

Scattered throughout the NE Area at Grouping, at more than twenty separate sheds, the class mainly stuck to the area bounded by the former NER system except for a couple which ventured to Glasgow in the mid 1920's and the wartime transfer of No.77 to Wrexham from 1940 to 1944. Up to the end of the J71 class they still worked the same duties at the same places where the class had initially been employed more than sixty years previously.

Withdrawals had started in 1933 but stopped shortly after the outbreak of war so that eighty-one J71 survived into BR days. Of these all but nine managed to gain their BR allotted numbers. The last four engines were condemned in February 1961 and that little group contained one of the elders of the class, No.68233 (LNER No.326 of 1887) which had served the railways for seventy-four years!

J72

The 6 inch smaller wheels and larger 17in x 24in. cylinders, fitted to the Wilson Worsdell version of the North Eastern Standard 0-6-0 shunting tank engine, along with a small number of minor detail alterations, set it apart from the Thomas Worsdell design. Classified E1 by the NER, it became LNER Class J72 and seventy-five of them entered LNER ownership. The first of them, No.462, was put into traffic in December 1898 along with nine others. During March and April of the following year another ten followed. Besides No.462 the other nineteen were all

The first ninety engines of Class J71, numbered randomly from 27 to 1314, were built at Darlington between November 1886 and August 1892. Note the single steel plate for the front buffer beam, also that no coal rails are fitted on the bunker.

Ten tank engines built at Darlington in December 1898 and numbered 462, 1715, 1718, 1721, 1722, 1732, 1744, 1746, 1761 and 1770, formed the genesis of LNER Class J72. Note the single steel plate buffer beam at both ends and the short bunker with three open coal rails.

numbered in the 17XX range. No more were built until fifteen years later when Vincent Raven had taken the helm and he had twenty E1's constructed during the latter months of 1914. The Raven version had a larger coal bunker, deeper frames, Ross 'pop' safety valves in place of the Ramsbottom type, and wooden sandwich bufferbeams replaced the steel plate variety of the original twenty engines. There were also a number of detail differences. The changes, along with the extra coal capacity, added nearly two tons to the Raven version. One other noticeable change made by Raven was the numbering of this batch which came out with a numerical sequence from 2173 to 2192 in order.

In 1920 ten more engines - 2303 to 2312 - joined the class from Darlington works, with another twenty-five - 2313 to 2337 - being supplied by an outside contractor shortly before Grouping. Another ten J72 came out during November and December 1925 but these were made at Doncaster albeit to the exact specification of the Raven version with no apparent Doncaster influences but the LNER had reverted to the haphazard numbering system used by most of the pre-Group companies and the ten new 0-6-0Ts carried numbers between 500 and 581. Under the 1946 renumbering scheme all the engines referred to above took the numbers 8670 to 8744 in construction order.

In 1946 the LNER published its five year plan for the construction of 1000 new locomotives, which were to be made up of ten standard classes. Although not at first identified, Class J72 was to be adopted for light shunting work and 65 were to be built, even though the design was some fifty years old. None actually appeared prior to nationalisation but in October 1949 Darlington works turned out the first of twenty-eight BR version J72's. These engines were based on the Raven version but had up-to-date LNER detail differences such as Group Standard buffers and drawgear (a number of the earlier engines had already had these fitted from the 1930's onward). The last of the BR-built J72's appeared in May 1951, nearly fifty three years after the class was first put into traffic by Wilson Worsdell.

As aluded to above, Class J72 shared the same boiler type as J71 and the Diagram 73 type's further history is added to here.

When Nos.2183, 2303, 2310 and 2312 were transferred to the Scottish Area in 1932 they were carrying boilers 8099, D1144, D1167 and D1177 respectively. The boilers were allotted Cowlairs numbers 1792 to 1795 in that order, but the renumbering took some years to be put into effect. Meanwhile further J72's were permanently transferred to Scotland but all kept their Darlington boiler numbers.

By the time that the BR boiler renumbering scheme began in September 1950, Diagram 73 boilers were in use only on classes J71 and J72. Darlington allotted numbers 25550 to 25691 to the engines in their care (i.e. not those in the Scottish Region). The new numbers were applied as and when each engine visited works for repair or overhaul, in the order of re-use, with no account being taken of either age or former number. Twenty-six new boilers were made at Darlington during 1951/2 and these took numbers 25692 to 25717.

The Scottish Region followed a different plan with their renumbering scheme. The thirteen Diagram 73 boilers on their books were allotted numbers 25790 to 25802 in December 1950, in order of age. As each one turned up at works it was given its pre-ordained number. It should be noted that boilers 25637 and 25670 were sent from Darlington to Inverurie in 1957 and 1953 respectively as replacements for scrapped boilers, but they kept their Darlington numbers.

New J72 Nos.69021 to 69028 were turned out in April/May 1951, after the BR numbering scheme was introduced. Three

of them took boilers numbered 25581, 25582 and 25583, but the other five had boilers which were included in the batch of the twenty-six replacement boilers mentioned earlier, as Nos.25694-25697 and 25699. Why there was a change of plan is not obvious. The new boilers were fitted in random order to the new engines. A final batch of thirty new boilers, numbered 25718 to 25747, were constructed in 1954/5.

In the meantime, renumbering of old boilers had reached 25691 in February 1954 but there were still a few yet to be done and these became 25748 to 25752. The last in May 1956 was fitted to J72 No.68715 which it carried to withdrawal in July 1961.

All the North Eastern engines and the ten LNER engines supplied by Doncaster, had steam brakes only from new but in 1937 two of the class were fitted with vacuum ejectors along with carriage warming equipment so that they could work on carriage shunting. No more were so fitted until the very end of the LNER when a start was made to fit thirteen of the class with vacuum ejectors and steam heating. Five more followed in 1950. Of the BR built J72's, only the last eight had vacuum ejectors and heating apparatus fitted from new, the first twenty were equipped with steam brake only. However, from 1953 five of these had vacuum ejectors fitted. This gear was taken off withdrawn J71 and J77 engines which had hitherto carried out much of the carriage shunting in the NE Region. Eighteen of the earlier engines were also fitted with vacuum ejectors from the same sources and it was not until February 1960 that the last one (68754) was equipped. By now withdrawals had started within J72 class; No.68718, of 1920 vintage, was the first to succumb, a mere thirty-seven years old. The newer engines varied in age from eleven to fifteen years when they were condemned. One of those, No.69023 was withdrawn in October 1964 and transferred to Departmental Stock where it became No.59, a transfer which was to see the 0-6-0T purchased for preservation, ensuring LNER Class J72 will live on. No.69005 was also transferred to Departmental Stock, as No.58, and when condemned in October 1967 was the last survivor in BR service.

Like the J71's, the J72 engines could be seen all over the former NER system by 1925 but whereas just a few J71 moved from the Area, quite a number of J72 were transferred away with eight going to Scotland, the majority of those moving as far north as Aberdeen. On the old Great Central system Bidston had three from 1930 until 1935 when one of those moved to Neasden until 1940 when it transferred back to Wirral where a few other J72 had since come and gone. Scotland was a temporary recipient early on when a single member of the class, No.1733 was tried at St Margarets during 1924. Some time later, from 1932 onwards, six ended up at Kittybrewster whilst Eastfield also had a couple from 1939. The latter pair in exchange for two condemned J71 which worked the trips between Cowlairs locomotive works and Eastfield shed. Four of the BR contingent were sent to Scotland after unpopular residencies on former Great Eastern territory but with the advent of the diesel shunter and the accelerating loss of traffic to road transport, the days of the 0-6-0T on BR were quickly coming to an end no matter how good the pedigree or longevity. So, another great class passed into history after a somewhat glorious but no frills existence.

For the next ten engines, built at Darlington between November 1892 and January 1893, Nos.1196 to 1199, 969, 972, 137, 977, 978 and 980, some second-hand material was used and all of them acquired previously used wheels. Those on No.978 were the normal 4ft 6in. but the other nine had only 4ft 0in. diameter. However, those on Nos.137 and 1196 had been changed to the standard size for the J71 class before Grouping.

Around 1900, three open coal rails were put on to the bunker, although odd ones only got two rails. From 1910 plating was put behind the rails.

The final twenty engines for the J71 class were built at Darlington between November 1894 and November 1895. They were numbered 1134, and then randomly between 1666 and 1864. All of these engines had 16³/₄ in. diameter cylinders instead of the 16in. of the earlier 100 engines. At Grouping all were in black livery.

Seven engines, Nos 969, 972, 977, 980, 1197, 1198 and 1199, still had 4ft 0in wheels when they got their LNER livery and No.969 still had them when withdrawn on 22nd September 1933. No.977 is known to have had them at least to December 1940 - *see* page 35, bottom - and no change was recorded for Nos.977, 980 and 1198 either.

CLASS J71

144

Darlington 11.

To traffic 11/1886.

REPAIRS:
???. ?/?—?/12/08.**G.**
???. ?/?—?/4/21.**?.**
Ghd. 10/10—5/12/23.**G.**
Ghd. 30/6—1/10/26.**G.**
Ghd. 20/12/27—10/2/28.**G.**
Ghd. 6/11—15/12/30.**G.**
Dar. 12/6—14/7/33.**H.**

BOILERS:
D490.
D1972 ?/12/08.
D2033 (new) 10/2/28.

SHEDS:
Tyne Dock.
Heaton 24/11/26. *On loan.*
Tyne Dock ?/?/?.
Consett 21/11/29.
Tyne Dock 15/2/35.

CONDEMNED: 15/5/37.
Into Dar. for cut up 30/11/37.

___

165

Darlington 12.

To traffic 11/1886.

REPAIRS:
???. ?/?—?/8/06.**G.**
???. ?/?—?/10/20.**?.**
Dar. 25/9—29/11/23.**G.**
Dar. 18/2—15/6/27.**G.**
Dar. 1/5—31/7/30.**G.**
Dar. 26/4—31/5/35.**G.**
Dar. 28/1—7/3/39.**G.**
Dar. 22/10—15/11/41.**G.**
Dar. 13/7—16/8/44.**G.**
Dar. 20/11/47—23/1/48.**G.**
Ghd. 17/9—6/10/51.**G.**
Ghd. 27/1—18/2/55.**G.**
Ghd. 23/2—11/3/55.**N/C.**
Dar. 18/1/60. *Not repaired.*

BOILERS:
D491.
D1859 ?/8/06.
D1952 (new) 15/6/27.
D984 (ex577) 31/5/35.

D1728 *(exJ72 2336)* 7/3/39.
  4589 *(exJ72 2190)* 15/11/41.
D1732 *(exJ72 500)* 16/8/44.
  2531 *(exJ72 8687)* 23/1/48.
  25714 (new) 6/10/51.
  25723 (new) 18/2/55.

SHEDS:
Middlesbrough.
York 9/10/34.
Hull Dairycoates 25/9/55.

RENUMBERED:
  8230 24/11/46.
  ᴇ**8230** 23/1/48.
  68230 6/10/51.

CONDEMNED: 25/1/60.
Cut up at Darlington.

___

299

Darlington 14.

To traffic 12/1886.

REPAIRS:
???. ?/?—?/1/04.**G.**
???. ?/?—?/2/22.**G.**
Dar. 18/2—14/5/27.**G.**
Dar. 6/7—12/8/32.**G.**
Dar. 6—15/6/34.**N/C.**
Spark arrestor fitted.
Dar. 29/9—27/10/37.**G.**
Dar. 14/11—7/12/40.**G.**
Dar. 30/9—23/10/43.**G.**
Dar. 10/5—6/6/46.**G.**
Dar.16/7/51. *Not repaired.*

BOILERS:
D493.
D1417 ?/1/04.
D1323 (new) ?/2/22.
D1336 *(exJ72 2309)* 27/10/37.
D1959 *(exJ72 1715)* 7/12/40.
HL102 (ex221) 23/10/43.
  8095 *(exJ72 581)* 6/6/46.

SHEDS:
Shildon.
Hull Dairycoates 9/10/34.
Starbeck 30/5/40.
York 28/7/46.
Darlington 17/7/49.

RENUMBERED:
8231 27/10/46.

CONDEMNED: 16/7/51.
Cut up at Darlington.

___

317

Darlington 16.

To traffic 12/1886.

REPAIRS:
???. ?/?—?/5/00.**G.**
???. ?/?—?/5/17.**G.**
???. ?/?—6/9/22.**G.**
Ghd. 30/12/24—28/2/25.**G.**
Ghd. 10/3—27/4/28.**G.**
Ghd. 21—23/5/28.**N/C.**
Ghd. 26/3—8/5/31.**G.**
Dar. 3/1/36. *Not repaired.*

BOILERS:
D495.
D1403 ?/5/00.
D657 (new) ?/5/17.

SHED:
Tyne Dock.

CONDEMNED: 13/5/36.
Cut up at Darlington.

___

261

Darlington 13.

To traffic 1/1887.

REPAIRS:
???. ?/?—?/10/08.**G.**
???. ?/?—?/4/21.**?.**
Dar. 14/1—21/5/27.**G.**
Dar. 22/6—24/8/31.**G.**
Dar. 31/8—20/10/34.**G.**
Dar. 27/10—25/11/39.**G.**
Dar. 31/3—30/4/43.**G.**
Dar. 28/5—20/6/46.**G.**
Ghd. 25/4—19/5/49.**G.**
Ghd. 14/1—6/2/53.**G.**

BOILERS:
D492.
D1967 ?/10/08.
D1950 (new) 21/5/27.
D1328 *(ex347)* 20/10/34.
D2004 *(exJ72 2311)* 25/11/39.
D2016 *(exJ72 576)* 30/4/43.
  2406 *(ex8315)* 20/6/46.

4587 *(exJ72 8708)* 19/5/49.
25667 6/2/53.

SHEDS:
Carlisle.
Hull Dairycoates 21/5/23.
Neville Hill 31/12/25.
Hull Dairycoates 12/2/26.

RENUMBERED:
  8232 10/11/46.
  68232 19/5/49.

CONDEMNED: 4/2/57.
Cut up at Darlington.

___

304

Darlington 15.

To traffic 1/1887.

REPAIRS:
???. ?/?—?/12/01.**G.**
???. ?/?—?/11/19.**G.**
Ghd. 9/2—28/4/23.**G.**
Ghd. 8—24/9/24.**L.**
Ghd. 8/7—15/10/26.**H.**
Ghd. 12/4—24/5/29.**G.**
Ghd. 9/11—16/12/32.**G.**

BOILERS:
D494.
D1407 ?/12/01.
  D974 (new) ?/11/19.

SHED:
West Hartlepool.

*Sold 19/2/36 to Cowpen Coal
Co. Ltd. & became Cambois
Colliery No.12. Scrapped 1954.*

___

399

Darlington 19.

To traffic 1/1887.

REPAIRS:
Dar. ?/?—?/5/08.**G.**
Vacuum ejector fitted 11-12/09.
Dar. 18/6—11/9/23.**G.**
Dar. 14/7—19/11/26.**G.**
Dar. 12/3—24/4/29.**G.**
Dar. 25/3—24/4/31.**G.**

___

WORKS CODES:- Cow - Cowlairs. Dar - Darlington. Don - Doncaster. Ghd - Gateshead. Gor - Gorton. Inv - Inverurie. Kit - Kittybrewster. RSH - Robert, Stephenson & Hawthorn. Str - Stratford. Yk - York.
REPAIR CODES:- **C/H** - Casual Heavy. **C/L** - Casual Light. **G** - General. **H**- Heavy. **H/I** - Heavy Intermediate. **L** - Light. **L/I** - Light Intermediate. **N/C** - Non-Classified.

The LNER did change three engines to the standard 4ft 6in. wheels:- Nos.1199 (12th June 1929), 1197 (23rd August 1935) and 972 (27th March 1936). Hull Outward yard, 1933.

All the original boilers, and replacements built prior to 1914, had Ramsbottom safety valves enclosed by the customary brass trumpet. This was a 1908 built boiler used by No.278 from December 1908 to October 1927.

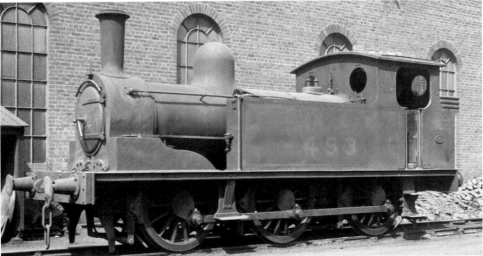

No.1688, in January 1915, was the first to have Ross 'pops' and these were then fitted on all subsequent boilers. Eastfield, July 1938.

Emission from safety valves bothered some crews (it obscured their view) who used various expedients to control it. This modified trumpet covered Ross 'pops' and not Ramsbottom valves as proved by the absence of a relieving lever across the top. Blaydon, August 1939.

No.285, one of the two based at Eastfield shed, was fitted with a separate shield to each of the 'pop' valves, and was so fitted at its 26th December 1936 withdrawal.

(below) This July 1954 photograph shows an unaltered Ramsbottom cover shield over 'pop' valves. Note that the chimney still has the inner rim. Borough Gardens, July 1954.

Due to corrosion, some had the inner rim turned off, No.68260 being another example and the top illustration on page 36 shows the effect of corrosion at the top of the chimney. Darlington, June 1955.

399 cont./
Dar. 22/3—5/4/32.**N/C.**

BOILERS:
D498.
D1951 ?/5/08.
  D708 (ex '44' 106) 19/11/26.
  D443 (exJ72 1742) 24/4/31.

SHED:
York.

CONDEMNED: 3/11/33.
Cut up at Darlington.

_____

27

Darlington 17.

To traffic 2/1887.

REPAIRS:
???. ?/?—?/6/06.**G.**
???. ?/?—?/3/12.**G.**
???. ?/?—.11/20.**?.**
Ghd. 12/6—13/8/23.**G.**
Dar. 16/12/26—10/2/27.**G.**
Dar. 27/8—22/10/29.**G.**

BOILERS:
  D496.
D1205 ?/6/06.
  D52 (new) ?/3/12.

SHEDS:
Darlington.
Hull Alexandra Dock 11/11/31.

CONDEMNED: 22/9/33.
Cut up at Darlington.

_____

326

Darlington 18.

To traffic 2/1887.

REPAIRS:
???. ?/?—?/12/01.**G.**
???. ?/?—?/4/18.**G.**
Ghd. 3/12/23—30/1/24.**G.**
Ghd. 16/11/26—31/1/27.**G.**
Ghd. 22/10—5/12/29.**G.**
Ghd. 13/10—9/11/32.**G.**
Dar. 3/2—4/3/38.**G.**
Dar. 11/12/41—8/1/42.**G.**
Dar. 28/6—11/8/45.**G.**
Dar. 27/8—17/9/48.**G.**
Ghd. 28/1—23/2/52.**H/I.**
Ghd. 7/5—1/6/56.**G.**

BOILERS:
  D497.

D1406 ?/12/01.
  D706 (new) ?/4/18.
  E21/9 (exJ72 2321) 9/11/32.
  E21/9 reno. AW 59 4/3/38.
  8090 (ex452) 8/1/42.
  8091 (exJ72 1720) 11/8/45.
  2833 (exJ72 8711) 17/9/48.
  2833 reno. 25626 23/2/52.
  25677 (exJ72 69011) 1/6/56.

SHEDS:
Tyne Dock.
West Hartlepool 9/10/34.

RENUMBERED:
  8233 27/10/46.
  68233 17/9/48.

CONDEMNED: 20/2/61.
Into Dar. for cut up 22/2/61.

_____

533

Darlington 20.

To traffic 2/1887.

REPAIRS:
???. ?/?—?/8/91.**G.**
???. ?/?—?/3/02.**G.**
???. ?/?—?/7/20.**G.**
Ghd. 30/5—27/7/23.**G.**
Ghd. 22/11—12/12/23.**L.**
Ghd. 29/12/26—4/3/27.**G.**
Ghd. 10/1—14/2/30.**G.**
Dar. 18/2—23/3/35.**G.**
Dar. 17/1—10/2/40.**G.**
Dar. 4/4—15/5/42.**L.**
Dar. 28/11—22/12/44.**G.**
Dar. 10/9—17/10/47.**G.**
Ghd. 25/9—13/10/50.**G.**

BOILERS:
  D499.
  D985 ?/8/91.
  D1409 ?/3/02.
  D981 (new) ?/7/20.
  D1320 (ex280) 23/3/35.
  2403 (ex248) 10/2/40.
  4592 (ex1140) 22/12/44.
  25562 (ex8257) 13/10/50.

SHEDS:
West Hartlepool.
West Auckland 27/5/40.
Gateshead 1/2/41.
Heaton 26/9/48.

RENUMBERED:
  8234 2/6/46.
  68234 13/10/50.

CONDEMNED: 2/8/54.
Cut up at Darlington.

70

Darlington 21.

To traffic 4/1887.

REPAIRS:
???. ?/?—?/9/05.**G.**
???. ?/?—?/11/21.**?.**
Ghd. 20/10—23/12/24.**G.**
Ghd. 3/7—5/9/28.**G.**
Dar. 28/7—12/9/33.**G.**
Wooden front buffer beam fitted.
Dar. 12/8—9/9/37.**N/C.**
Dar. 25/5—15/6/38.**N/C.**
Dar. 13/12/40—10/1/41.**G.**
GS buffers & hook fitted.
Dar. 26/1—18/2/44.**G.**
Dar. 4—28/11/47.**G.**
Ghd. 25/2—6/4/48.**L.**
After collision.
Ghd. 4/2—1/3/52.**H/I.**
Dar. 17—27/9/56.**C/L.**
Dar. 15/1—8/2/57.**G.**
Dar. 6—8/3/57.**N/C.**

BOILERS:
  D521.
D1852 ?/9/05.
  D1707 (new) 23/12/24.
  8096 (exJ72 1722) 10/1/41.
  4588 (exJ72 2181) 18/2/44.
  8089 (exJ72 8746) 28/11/47.
  8089 reno. 25627 1/3/52.
  25658 (exJ72 69005) 8/3/57.

SHEDS:
Borough Gardens.
Darlington 5/12/38.
West Auckland 11/5/58.

RENUMBERED:
  8235 26/5/46.
  68235 6/4/48.

CONDEMNED: 7/11/60.
Into Dar. for cut up 8/11/60.

_____

168

Darlington 22.

To traffic 4/1887.

REPAIRS:
???. ?/?—?/3/06.**G.**
???. ?/?—?/5/10.**G.**
Dar. 17/7—29/11/23.**G.**
Dar. 31/10/27—14/1/28.**G.**
Dar. 29/6—9/8/32.**G.**
Dar. 7/2—16/3/38.**G.**
Dar. 9/9—3/10/42.**G.**
Dar. 15/3—13/4/46.**G.**
Ghd. 3/2—7/3/50.**G.**

BOILERS:
D522.
D749 ?/3/06.
D2051 ?/5/10.
  D2032 (new) 14/1/28.
  8093 (ex179) 16/3/38.
  2408 (ex1123) 3/10/42.
  D2027 (ex572) 13/4/46.
  8110 (ex8259) 7/3/50.

SHEDS:
Darlington.
Darlington North Road 28/5/32.

RENUMBERED:
  8236 22/12/46.
  68236 7/3/50.

CONDEMNED: 1/11/55.
Cut up at Darlington.

_____

263

Darlington 23.

To traffic 4/1887.

REPAIRS:
???. ?/?—?/6/06.**G.**
Dar. 8/7—16/10/23.**G.**
Dar. 7/5—27/7/27.**G.**
Dar. 8/9—2/10/31.**G.**

BOILERS:
  D529.
D1857 ?/6/06.
D1959 (new) 27/7/27.

SHED:
Darlington North Road.
Service Stock until 8/26.

CONDEMNED: 15/5/37.
Into Dar. for cut up 30/11/37.

_____

272

Darlington 24.

To traffic 5/1887.

REPAIRS:
???. ?/?—?/3/08.**G.**
Ghd. 8/10—19/12/24.**G.**
Ghd. 31/8—12/10/28.**G.**
Ghd. 2/3—6/4/32.**G.**
Dar. 7—28/1/39.**G.**
Dar. 9/9—4/10/41.**G.**
Dar. 15/9—7/10/44.**G.**
Dar. 16/5/47. *Not repaired.*

BOILERS:
D530.

The original buffer type was the parallel shank with hollow spindle, and some kept this variety to withdrawal.

Some changed to taper shank with an end collar and a solid spindle. Both this and the earlier type had a circular flange. West Hartlepool, April 1939.

By the late 1920's Group Standard buffers and draw hook began to be fitted and these buffers had a square flange. York.

Although No. 68306 did not get Group Standard buffers it was changed to a G.S. drawhook. To adjust for its extra length, wood packings were fitted between the buffer flanges and the buffer beam. Gateshead.

(above) **Originally a single steel plate front buffer beam was fitted, and No.285 only changed to wood sandwich type - *see* page 7, top - when ex works 5th January 1933, at its last repair. Eastfield.**

By Grouping, the majority had been changed, at the front end only, to the wood sandwich type, the buffer type being irrelevant. Darlington.

No.68260 kept its single plate buffer beam to its 7th March 1960 withdrawal, despite being one of those fitted with Group Standard buffers and hook. The only other J71 so noted was No.68264.

272 cont./
D1947 ?/3/08.
D1339 *(new)* 19/12/24.
  4588 *(ex1862)* 28/1/39.
  2524 *(exJ72 2325)* 4/10/41.
  3508 *(new)* 7/10/44.

SHEDS:
Blaydon.
Hull Dairycoates 9/10/34.
Heaton 12/5/42.

RENUMBERED:
8237 24/11/46.

CONDEMNED: 5/7/47.
Cut up at Darlington.

278

Darlington 25.

To traffic 5/1887.

REPAIRS:
???. ?/?—?/8/03.**G.**
???. ?/?—?/12/08.**G.**
Dar. 23/5—5/8/24.**G.**
Dar. 19/10—31/12/27.**G.**
Dar. 10/11/31—8/1/32.**G.**

BOILERS:
D531.
D796 ?/8/03.
D1969 ?/12/08.
D2030 *(new)* 31/12/27.

SHEDS:
Neville Hill.
Starbeck 24/12/29.

CONDEMNED: 20/11/35.
Into Dar. for cut up 8/11/35.

347

Darlington 26.

To traffic 5/1887.

REPAIRS:
???. ?/?—?/9/07.**G.**
???. ?/?—?/12/22.**G.**
Dar. 22/9—30/11/25.**G.**
Dar. 21/8—11/10/28.**G.**
Dar. 31/3—8/5/31.**G.**
Dar. 11/7—31/8/34.**G.**
Dar. 6/10—2/11/38.**G.**
Dar. 4—9/11/38.**N/C.**
Dar. 11/12/40—2/1/41.**G.**
Dar. 26/4—17/5/44.**G.**
Dar. 5/5—6/6/47.**G.**
Ghd. 4/5—2/6/50.**G.**

Dar. 13/4—8/5/54.**C/L.**

BOILERS:
D532.
D1414 ?/9/07.
D1328 *(new)* ?/12/22.
AW66 [exE21/16]
(exJ72 2328) 31/8/34.
  2849 *(new)* 2/11/38.
  8087 *(exJ72 2318)* 2/1/41.
  2395 *(exJ72 2327)* 17/5/44.
  8104 *(exJ72 8680)* 6/6/47.
  4062 *(new)* 2/6/50.

SHEDS:
Hull Alexandra Dock.
York 1/7/24.
Normanton 12/6/37.
On loan to LM Region 1/1/52.
To LMR (Normanton) 6/9/53.

RENUMBERED:
8238 15/12/46.
68238 2/6/50.

CONDEMNED: 5/9/55.
Cut up at Darlington 9/55.

493

Darlington 27.

To traffic 6/1887.

REPAIRS:
???. ?/?—?/6/06.**G.**
Dar. 18/2—29/4/25.**G.**
Dar. 15/10—26/11/28.**G.**
Dar. 3—27/4/34.**G.**
Dar. 20/3/39. *Not repaired.*

BOILERS:
D533.
D1856 ?/6/06.
D1732 *(new)* 29/4/25.
D1322 *(ex254)* 27/4/34.

SHEDS:
Hull Alexandra Dock.
Hull Dairycoates 12/6/39.

CONDEMNED: 29/7/39.
Cut up at Darlington.

494

Darlington 28.

To traffic 6/1887.

REPAIRS:
???. ?/?—?/9/09.**G.**
Dar. 17/4—8/7/24.**G.**

Dar. 3/10—15/11/28.**G.**
Dar. 19/7—21/8/34.**G.**
New front wooden buffer beam.
Dar. 30/10—29/11/39.**G.**
GS buffers & hook fitted.
Dar. 2/7—18/8/43.**G.**
Dar. 21/8/43.**N/C.**
Dar. 22/8—18/9/47.**G.**
Ghd. 11/2—1/3/52.**G.**
Ghd. 3—6/3/52.**N/C.**

BOILERS:
D535.
D2000 ?/9/09.
  8089 *(new)* 15/11/28.
AW57 *(exJ72 1744)* 29/11/39.
  2405 *(exJ72 1742)* 18/8/43.
  8086 *(exJ72 8685)* 18/9/47.
25613 1/3/52.

SHEDS:
Middlesbrough.
Darlington 18/11/38.

RENUMBERED:
8239 3/11/46.
68239 1/3/52.

CONDEMNED: 23/11/56.
Cut up at Darlington.

499

Darlington 29.

To traffic 6/1887.

REPAIRS:
???. ?/?—?/12/06.**G.**
Dar. 26/8—25/10/24.**G.**
Dar. 31/1—21/3/29.**G.**
Dar. 25/3—25/4/31.**G.**
Vacuum ejector fitted.
Dar. 6/8—29/9/34.**G.**
Dar. 30/1—2/3/37.**G.**
Vacuum drain pipe fitted.
Dar. 2/2—18/3/40.**G.**
Dar. 29/4—22/5/42.**G.**
Dar. 25/5—21/6/44.**G.**
Dar. 4/1—2/2/46.**G.**
Dar. 9—25/6/48.**G.**
Dar. 1—26/8/50.**C/L.**
Ghd. 5/7—10/8/51.**G.**
Dar. 12—21/2/52.**C/H.**
Ghd. 26/4—21/5/54.**G.**
Dar. 8/9/56. *Not repaired.*

BOILERS:
D536.
D1413 ?/12/06.
D1331 *(new)* 25/10/24.
  2868 *(new)* 2/3/37.
  7962 *(exJ72 500)* 18/3/40.
  3272 *(new)* 22/5/42.

2868 *(exJ72 1733)* 2/2/46.
  4585 *(ex8256)* 25/6/48.
25604 10/8/51.
25564 *(exJ72 68740)* 21/5/54.

SHEDS:
Hull Alexandra Dock.
Normanton 1/7/24.
York 8/12/32.

RENUMBERED:
8240 15/12/46.
68240 25/6/48.

CONDEMNED: 10/9/56.
Cut up at Darlington.

811

Darlington 30.

To traffic 6/1887.

REPAIRS:
???. ?/?—2/7/09.**G.**
Vacuum ejector fitted 11-12/09.
???. ?/?—?/5/22.**?.**
Ghd. 17/12/24—13/2/25.**G.**
Ghd. 15/10—12/12/27.**G.**
Vacuum ejector removed.
Ghd. 18/3—21/4/31.**G.**

BOILERS:
D537.
D1991 ?/7/09.
D2018 *(new)* 12/12/27.

SHEDS:
Gateshead.
Tyne Dock 29/8/34.

CONDEMNED: 15/5/37.
Into Dar. for cut up 10/12/37.

242

Darlington 41.

To traffic 4/1888.

REPAIRS:
???. ?/?—?/7/06.**G.**
???. ?/?—?/2/22.**?.**
Ghd. 6/1—31/3/26.**G.**
Ghd. 12/10—19/11/28.**G.**
Ghd. 13/8—9/9/30.**L.**
After collision.
Ghd. 4/4—3/5/32.**G.**
Dar. 25/2—27/3/35.**L.**
After collision.
Dar. 23/9/36. *Not repaired.*

242 cont./
BOILERS:
D610.
D1858 ?/7/06.
D1729 *(new)* 31/3/26.

SHED:
Blaydon.

CONDEMNED: 9/10/36.
Cut up at Darlington.

268

Darlington 42.

To traffic 4/1888.

REPAIRS:
???. ?/?—?/6/08.**G.**
Ghd. 16/8—9/10/24.**G.**
Ghd. 14/10—30/11/27.**G.**
Ghd. 19/6—31/7/31.**G.**
Dar. 11/8/39. *Not repaired.*

BOILERS:
D611.
D1954 ?/6/08.
D2013 *(new)* 30/11/27.

SHED:
Blaydon.

CONDEMNED: 12/8/39.
Cut up at Darlington.

275

Darlington 43.

To traffic 4/1888.

REPAIRS:
???. ?/?—?/10/09.**G.**
Ghd. 21/9—15/11/23.**G.**
Ghd. 8/4—18/7/27.**G.**
Ghd. 13/11—4/12/28.**H.**
Ghd. 1—17/7/30.**L.**
Vacuum ejector fitted.
Ghd. 14/8—15/9/31.**G.**
Ghd. 29/4—6/5/32.**L.**
Dar. 14/11—8/12/34.**G.**
Dar. 2/12/37—28/1/38.**G.**
Dar. 1—24/6/40.**G.**
Dar. 16/12/42—13/1/43.**G.**
Dar. 23/1—17/2/45.**G.**
Dar. 16/5/47. *Not repaired.*

BOILERS:
D612.
D2015 ?/10/09.
8094 *(new)* 4/12/28.
8113 *(ex1134)* 8/12/34.

D2033 *(ex144)* 28/1/38.
8105 *(exJ72 1736)* 24/6/40.
D2026 *(exJ72 574)* 17/2/45.

SHED:
Heaton.

RENUMBERED:
8241 5/1/47.

CONDEMNED: 5/7/47.
Cut up at Darlington.

285

Darlington 44.

To traffic 5/1888.

REPAIRS:
???. ?/?—?/10/08.**G.**
Ghd. 18/8—10/10/23.**G.**
Ghd. 4/8—22/3/27.**G.**
Dar. 29/11/32—5/1/33.**G.**
New wood bufferbeam fitted.
Dar. 30/11/36. *Not repaired.*

BOILERS:
D613.
D1968 ?/10/08.
D1943 *(new)* 22/3/27.

SHEDS:
Carlisle.
Eastfield *by* 3/9/26.

CONDEMNED: 26/12/36.
Cut up at Darlington.

286

Darlington 45.

To traffic 5/1888.

REPAIRS:
???. ?/?—?/5/10.**G.**
Hls. ?/?—?/5/24.**H.**
Dar. 21/12/26—28/3/27.**G.**
Dar. 26/3—24/5/29.**G.**
Dar. 6/8—7/9/34.**G.**
Dar. 17/5—23/6/39.**G.**
Dar. 8/9—5/10/43.**G.**
Dar. 24/10—23/11/46.**G.**
Dar. 24/1—15/2/47.**L.**
Ghd. 28/10—23/11/49.**G.**
Ghd. 28—29/11/49.**N/C.**
Ghd. 8/3—2/4/54.**G.**
Dar. 29/7/58. *Not repaired.*

BOILERS:
D614.
D2056 ?/5/10.

8103 *(new)* 24/5/29.
AW74 *(ex453)* 23/6/39.
D1171 *(exJ72 2173)* 5/10/43.
D2015 *(exJ72 8694)* 23/11/46.
HL99 *(ex8299)* 23/11/49.
25597 *(exJ72 68708)* 2/4/54.

SHEDS:
Hull Alexandra Dock.
Hull Dairycoates 12/6/39.
Stockton 10/4/55.
West Auckland 26/6/55.

RENUMBERED:
8242 23/11/46.
68242 23/11/49.

CONDEMNED: 4/8/58.
Cut up at Darlington.

403

Darlington 46.

To traffic 5/1888.

REPAIRS:
???. ?/?—?/1/06.**G.**
Ghd. 26/5—9/8/23.**G.**
Ghd. 11/11/26—28/1/27.**G.**
Ghd. 20/11—31/12/29.**G.**
Ghd. 29/5—19/6/30.**N/C.**
Vacuum ejector fitted.
Ghd. 20—31/5/32.**N/C.**
Dar. 9/4—3/5/34.**G.**
Dar. 30/4—12/7/35.**H.**
Dar. 3/5—10/8/39.**G.**
Dar. 7/9—1/10/42.**G.**
Dar. 6/3—6/4/45.**G.**
Dar. 6/12/47—14/1/48.**G.**

BOILERS:
D615.
D1854 ?/1/06.
D1334 *(new)* 9/8/23.
4585 *(ex577)* 10/8/39.
D1948 *(ex450)* 1/10/42.
AW71 *(exJ72 8702)* 14/1/48.

SHED:
Heaton.

RENUMBERED:
8243 8/12/46.

CONDEMNED: 2/3/50.
Cut up at Darlington.

541

Darlington 47.

To traffic 6/1888.

REPAIRS:
???. ?/?—?/12/08.**G.**
Ghd. 10/1—14/3/23.**G.**
Ghd. 11/5—29/9/27.**G.**
Ghd. 19/3—24/4/31.**G.**
Dar. 27/6—8/8/36.**G.**
Dar. 10/12/40—7/1/41.**G.**
Dar. 31/1—3/3/45.**G.**
Dar. 8/1—6/2/48.**G.**
Dar. 8—26/1/51.**G.**
Ghd. 27/9—22/10/54.**L/I.**
Dar. 22/3/58. *Not repaired.*

BOILERS:
D616.
D1971 ?/12/08.
D1995 *(new)* 29/9/27.
2839 *(exJ72 1721)* 7/1/41.
2872 *(exJ72 1721)* 3/3/45.
D1948 *(ex8243)* 6/2/48.
25578 26/1/51.

SHEDS:
East Hartlepool.
West Hartlepool 17/4/39.

RENUMBERED:
8244 16/6/46.
ᴇ**8244** 6/2/48.
68244 26/1/51.

CONDEMNED: 7/4/58.
Cut up at Darlington.

584

Darlington 48.

To traffic 6/1888.

REPAIRS:
???. ?/?—?/7/09.**G.**
Ghd. 30/1—10/4/23.**G.**
Ghd. 16/12/26—2/2/27.**G.**
Ghd. 19—28/5/27.**L.**
Ghd. 15/11—7/12/28.**H.**
Ghd. 26/3—6/5/31.**G.**
Dar. 29/1/35. *Not repaired.*

BOILERS:
D617.
D1996 ?/7/09.
8095 *(new)* 7/12/28.

SHED:
Tyne Dock.

CONDEMNED: 5/2/35.
Cut up at Darlington.

Nos.1197 and 1199 also had wood dumb buffers so that they could deal with chaldron type coal wagons, and they were still so fitted in the late 1930's.

For additional platform clearance on its passenger pilot duties at York station, No.1167 (only) needed one end of its single plate buffer beam trimming to avoid being bent forward as shown.

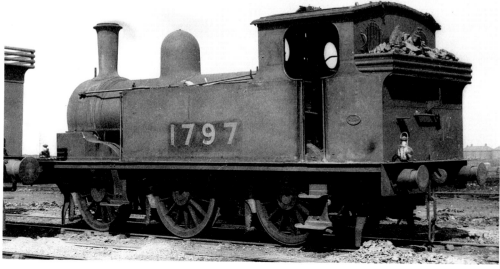

Rear buffer beams were all single steel plate and remained so throughout.

For shunting at Shildon wagon works, five J71's, Nos. 50, 241, 299, 802 and 977 were fitted at both front corners with shunting poles. These enabled wagons on adjacent lines to be moved when required. West Auckland, August 1936.

No.68255 (ex 241) retained the shunting poles until it was withdrawn on 18th August 1952. West Auckland, March 1951.

(below) The shunting poles had been taken off No.68254 (ex 50) when it was ex Gateshead works 13th October 1951 but the brackets for them could still be seen. Gateshead, July 1954.

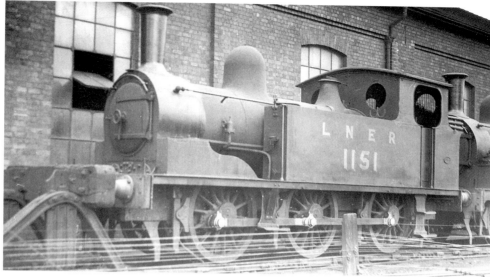

The first eighteen built, Nos.144, 165, 299, 317, 261, 304, 399, 27, 326, 533, 70, 168, 263, 272, 278, 347,493, and 494, had their frames cut square at the ends, thus coming well below the buffer beams. This was to take oak planks as buffers for moving chaldron wagons. Some of the engines built in 1892, including those using up second-hand parts, also had frames of this type.

Beginning with No.499, built in June 1887, the frame ends were cut away in an arc to where the guard irons were attached. Apart from the reversion in 1892, this was then the standard pattern. Only one deviation was noted; on No.165 (68230) at the rear end, the cut-away was straight instead of curved.

These deep, square ended, frames lasted into the 1950's, Nos.68233, 68235, 68238, 68239, 68291, 68298 and 68300 all being so noted. Normanton, April 1953.

From December 1909 the standard whistle was a single organ pipe mounted in front of the cab.

1123

Darlington 49.

To traffic 6/1888.

REPAIRS:
???. ?/?—?/5/03.**G.**
???. ?/?—?/7/19.**G.**
Ghd. 7/8—6/10/24.**G.**
Ghd. 20/9—25/11/27.**G.**
Ghd. 24/3—28/4/31.**G.**
Ghd. 26/11/34—12/1/35.**G.**
Dar. 15/2—23/3/39.**G.**
Dar. 11/8—5/9/42.**G.**
Dar. 16/10—10/11/45.**G.**
Dar. 12/6—18/7/47.**L.**
Dar. 20/10—12/11/48.**G.**
Ghd. 1—20/10/51.**G.**
Ghd. 10/12/54—13/1/55.**G.**
Dar. 23/4/59. *Not repaired.*

BOILERS:
D618.
D1416 ?/5/03.
  D69 *(ex'44' 46)* ?/7/19.
  2408 *(new)* 28/4/31.
  7960 *(ex280)* 5/9/42.
  2409 *(ex161)* 10/11/45.
  2538 *(exJ72 8704)* 12/11/48.
  25594 20/10/51.
  25719 *(new)* 13/1/55.

SHEDS:
Heaton.
Middlesbrough 1/5/55.
Thornaby 1/6/58.

RENUMBERED:
  8245 10/3/46.
  68245 12/11/48.

CONDEMNED: 27/4/59.
Cut up at Darlington.

1163

Darlington 50.

To traffic 6/1888.

REPAIRS:
???. ?/?—?/9/07.**G.**
???. ?/?—?/4/15.**G.**
Dar. ?/?—?/8/21.**L.**
Westinghouse brake fitted 6/22.
Dar. 21/2—29/5/25.**G.**
Dar. 22/5—30/7/29.**G.**
*Westinghouse equipment
removed. Steam brake refitted.*

BOILERS:
D619.
D1202 ?/9/07.

D445 *(new)* ?/4/15.

SHEDS:
York.
East Hartlepool 28/6/29.

CONDEMNED: 20/10/33.
Cut up at Darlington.

84

Darlington 81.

To traffic 7/1889.

REPAIRS:
???. ?/?—?/5/04.**G.**
???. ?/?—?/3/15.**G.**
???. ?/?—?/7/21.**?.**
Ghd. 25/8—18/11/25.**G.**
Ghd. 18/4—30/5/29.**G.**

BOILERS:
D749.
D1420 ?/5/04.
  D433 *(new)* ?/3/15.

SHEDS:
East Hartlepool.
West Hartlepool 25/3/29.

CONDEMNED: 9/8/33.
Cut up at Darlington.

1167

Darlington 82.

To traffic 7/1889.

REPAIRS:
Vacuum ejector fitted 11-12/09.
???. ?/?—?/7/10.**G.**
Dar. 25/4—26/7/23.**G.**
Dar. 14/10—22/12/25.**G.**
Dar. 26/4—27/6/29.**G.**
Dar. 9/12/31—3/2/32.**G.**
Dar. 12/12/33—16/1/34.**G.**
Dar. 1/10—13/11/35.**H.**
Dar. 29/6—16/8/37.**G.**
Dar. 29/5—19/6/40.**G.**
Dar. 24/3—15/4/44.**G.**
Dar. 7/1—2/2/46.**G.**
Ghd. 23/3—22/4/49.**G.**
Ghd. 7/1—1/2/52.**G.**
Ghd. 15/11—10/12/54.**G.**
Dar. 18/11/58. *Not repaired.*

BOILERS:
D758.
D2059 *(new)* ?/7/10.
  8109 *(new)* 27/6/29.
E21/11 *(exJ72 2323)* 16/1/34.

E21/11 *reno.AW61 13/11/35.*
D1949 *(exJ72 1736)* 16/8/37.
AW69 *(exJ72 2330)* 19/6/40.
  2538 *(ex1796)* 15/4/44.
D1943 *(exJ72 2189)* 2/2/46.
  7960 *(ex8275)* 22/4/49.
  25611 1/2/52.
  25579 *(ex68262)* 10/12/54.

SHED:
York.

RENUMBERED:
  8246 17/2/46.
  68246 22/4/49.

CONDEMNED: 24/11/58.
Cut up at Darlington.

221

Darlington 83.

To traffic 7/1889.

REPAIRS:
???. ?/?—?/3/10.**G.**
???. ?/?—?/12/20.**?.**
Ghd. 18/11/25—1/2/26.**G.**
Ghd. 5/5—11/6/30.**G.**
Dar. 1—27/10/34.**G.**
Dar. 18/10—20/11/39.**G.**
Dar. 20/9—12/10/43.**G.**
Dar. 22/11/47—12/2/48.**G.**
Dar. 15/8/51. *Not repaired.*

BOILERS:
D750.
D2053 ?/3/10.
HL902 *(new)* 11/6/30.
HL902 *reno.HL102 27/10/34.*
  HL95 *(exJ72 1734)* 12/10/43.
D1952 *(ex8298)* 12/2/48.

SHEDS:
Gateshead.
Heaton 23/7/50.

RENUMBERED:
  8247 5/5/46.
  ᴇ**8247** 12/2/48.

CONDEMNED: 15/8/51.
Cut up at Darlington.

224

Darlington 84.

To traffic 8/1889.

REPAIRS:
???. ?/?—?/4/10.**G.**

???. ?/?—?/3/21.**?.**
Ghd. 7/7—25/9/25.**G.**
Ghd. 30/8—16/12/29.**G.**
Ghd. 11/2—10/3/37.**G.**
New wood bufferbeam fitted.
Dar. 2/9—4/10/40.**G.**
Dar. 10/1—3/2/44.**G.**
Dar. 1/3—2/4/48.**G.**
Dar. 3—18/12/48.**L.**
Dar. 3/7/51. *Not repaired.*

BOILERS:
D751.
D2054 *(new)* ?/4/10.
HL889 *(new)* 16/12/29.
HL889 *reno.HL89 10/3/37.*
D2001 *(ex244)* 4/10/40.
  2540 *(exJ72 1763)* 3/2/44.
D1947 *(ex 8280)* 2/4/48.

SHEDS:
East Hartlepool.
West Hartlepool 25/3/29.

RENUMBERED:
  8248 5/5/46.
  68248 2/4/48.

CONDEMNED: 3/7/51.
Cut up at Darlington.

225

Darlington 85.

To traffic 8/1889.

REPAIRS:
???. ?/?—?/12/08.**G.**
Hls. ?/?—?/2/24.**H.**
Dar. 12/10—22/12/27.**G.**
Dar. 10/10—9/11/32.**G.**
Dar. 9/11/32—15/6/34
In store Darlington Paint Shop.
Dar. 15—16/6/34.**N/C.**
Fitted with spark arrestor.

BOILERS:
D752.
D1970 ?/12/08.
D2020 *(new)* 22/12/27.

SHED:
Hull Alexandra Dock.

CONDEMNED: 15/5/37.
Into Dar. for cut up 10/12/37.

Hartlepool based Nos.177, 181 and 403, from October 1920, were allowed to retain or revert to, the higher pitch bell shape whistle.

In LNER days it was mainly Heaton shedded engines which had bell-shaped whistles, some of them with the larger size. Heaton, May 1935.

(below) Darlington shedded No.68279, as shown, was out on 30th March 1951 from its final repair. It had a standard organ pipe and also a rim to its chimney. Darlington, April 1951.

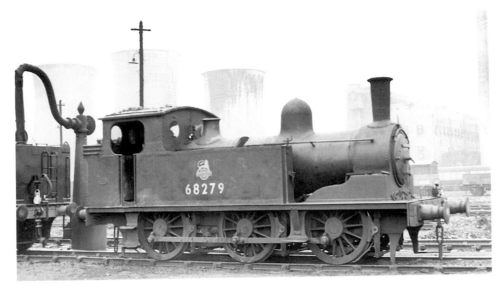

As a result of alteration at the shed, by May 1955, No.68279 had changed to a small bell-shape whistle and had the inner rim to the chimney turned off. Darlington, May 1955.

(above) Although Nos.285 and 453 went to Eastfield shed in 1926, to work as the shed and Cowlairs works yard shunters, neither was ever fitted with either long rear steps or rails on the bunker, characteristic of NBR shunting engines.

The original fastening for the smokebox door was by a pair of handles and many were always so fitted.

453

Darlington 86.

To traffic 8/1889.

REPAIRS:
???. ?/?—?/5/08.**G**.
Ghd. 8/11/23—8/1/24.**G**.
Ghd. 11/5—8/7/27.**G**.
Ghd. 17/12/31—26/1/32.**G**.
Ghd. 30/3—12/4/32.**L**.
Dar. 21/10—25/11/35.**G**.
Dar. 23/2/39. *Not repaired*.

BOILERS:
D753.
D1952 ?/5/08.
D1330 *(new)* 8/1/24.
AW74 [exE21/24]
(exJ72 2336) 25/11/35.

SHEDS:
Carlisle.
Eastfield *by* 8/26.

CONDEMNED: 25/2/39.
Cut up at Darlington.

492

Darlington 87.

To traffic 8/1889.

REPAIRS:
???. ?/?—?/9/09.**G**.
Dar. 12/12/23—17/3/24.**G**.
Dar. 15/6—29/9/26.**G**.
Dar. 17/10—23/12/27.**G**.
Dar. 29/10—28/11/30.**G**.
Dar. 18/10—14/11/34.**G**.
Dar. 25/6—24/7/40.**G**.
GS buffers & hook fitted.
Dar. 15/1—10/2/42.**G**.
Dar. 16/5—3/6/44.**G**.
Dar. 12/2—11/3/48.**G**.
Ghd. 29/12/52. *Not repaired*.

BOILERS:
D754.
D2011 ?/9/09.
D2022 *(new)* 23/12/27.
D2010 *(ex1084)* 14/11/34.
D128 *(ex338)* 24/7/40.
D2006 *(exJ72 1715)* 3/6/44.

SHEDS:
Starbeck.
Neville Hill 13/2/35.
Darlington 25/9/36.
Darlington North Rd 5/1/37.
Darlington ?/?/?.
West Auckland 28/7/46.

RENUMBERED:
8249 24/11/46.
E8249 11/3/48.

CONDEMNED: 5/1/53.
Cut up at Darlington.

495

Darlington 88.

To traffic 9/1889.

REPAIRS:
???. ?/?—?/3/99.**G**.
???. ?/?—?/10/10.**G**.
Ghd. 28/2—30/4/25.**G**.
Ghd. 9/5—6/7/28.**G**.
Dar. 27/2—27/3/29.**H**.
Vacuum ejector fitted.
Dar. 20/11—29/12/31.**G**.
Dar. 27/9—1/11/35.**G**.
Dar. 19/10—26/11/38.**G**.
Dar. 17/10—14/11/42.**G**.
Dar. 15/11—8/12/45.**G**.
Dar. 28/2—30/4/48.**G**.
Ghd. 28/9—20/10/50.**G**.
Ghd. 17/11—6/12/52.**G**.
Ghd. 28/6—29/7/55.**G**.
Dar. 10/3/59. *Not repaired*.

BOILERS:
D755.
D987 ?/3/99.
D2083 *(new)* ?/10/10.
HL8100 *(new)* 27/3/29.
  8101 *(ex237)* 1/11/35.
  8088 *(ex447)* 26/11/38.
  8107 *(exJ72 2191)* 14/11/42.
  AW70 *(ex1134)* 8/12/45.
  25561 *(exJ72 8735)* 20/10/50.
  25652 6/12/52.
  25730 *(new)* 29/7/55.

SHEDS:
West Hartlepool.
Selby 5/4/29.
York 14/5/30.

RENUMBERED:
8250 30/12/46.
68250 30/4/48.

CONDEMNED: 6/4/59.
Cut up at Darlington.

496

Darlington 89.

To traffic 9/1889.

REPAIRS:
???. ?/?—?/1/09.**G**.
Dar. 12/11/23—30/1/24.**G**.
Dar. 8/10—22/12/27.**G**.
Dar. 23/5—14/6/28.**N/C**.
Dar. 13/5—26/6/31.**G**.

BOILERS:
D756.
D1974 ?/1/09.
D2021 *(new)* 22/12/27.

SHEDS:
Darlington.
Hull Alexandra Dock 10/8/33.

CONDEMNED: 15/5/37.
Cut up at Darlington.

501

Darlington 90.

To traffic 9/1889.

REPAIRS:
???. ?/?—?/11/09.**G**.
Vacuum ejector fitted.
Ghd. 4/12/23—1/2/24.**G**.
Ghd. 30/12/26—24/3/27.**G**.
Ghd. 13/12/28—15/1/29.**H**.
Ghd. 19/9—29/10/30.**G**.
Ghd. 25/2—5/3/32.**L**.
GS buffers & hook fitted.
Dar. 17/7—24/8/34.**G**.
Dar. 23/9—29/10/37.**G**.
Dar. 15/5—12/6/40.**G**.
Dar. 13/2—11/3/41.**L**.
Dar. 21/5—1/7/43.**G**.
Dar. 16/8—12/9/45.**G**.
Dar. 4/12/47—2/1/48.**G**.
Ghd. 29/10—17/11/51.**H/I**.
Dar. 20—24/1/56. *Not Repaired. Sent to Gateshead Wks*.
Ghd. 26/1—17/2/56.**G**.
Dar. 6/1/59. *Not repaired*.

BOILERS:
D757.
D2016 ?/11/09.
  8096 *(new)* 15/1/29.
AW73 *(exJ72 2191)* 29/10/37.
HL93 *(ex1197)* 1/7/43.
  4586 *(ex450)* 12/9/45.
D1732 *(ex8230)* 2/1/48.
D1732 reno.25616 17/11/51.
  25664 *(exJ72 69006)* 17/2/56.

SHEDS:
Borough Gardens.
Gateshead 29/5/33.
Heaton 29/11/53.
Hull Dairycoates 7/4/57.
Hull Botanic Gardens 7/7/57.

Hull Dairycoates 29/9/57.

RENUMBERED:
8251 23/6/46.
68251 17/11/51.

CONDEMNED: 12/1/59.
Cut up at Darlington.

1083

Darlington 112.

To traffic 5/1890.

REPAIRS:
???. ?/?—?/9/06.**G**.
Dar. 29/7—10/10/24.**G**.
Dar. 3/8—28/9/28.**G**.
Dar. 24/5—16/6/32.**G**.
Dar. 10/7—17/8/35.**G**.
Dar. 28/3—23/4/40.**G**.
Dar. 29/9—19/10/42.**L**.
Short of water.
Dar. 1—26/4/44.**G**.
Dar. 6—28/11/47.**G**.
Ghd. 15/11—8/12/50.**G**.
Ghd. 11—19/12/50.**N/C**.
Ghd. 22/2—20/3/54.**G**.

BOILERS:
D790.
D1861 ?/9/06.
D1336 *(new)* 10/10/24.
D713 *(exJ72 1736)* 16/6/32.
AW55 [exE21/5]
(exJ72 2317) 17/8/35.
  2527 *(exJ72 2306)* 19/10/42.
  4582 *(exJ72 2325)* 26/4/44.
D1995 *(ex8316)* 28/11/47.
  4581 *(ex8284)* 8/12/50.
  25566 *(ex68282)* 20/3/54.

SHEDS:
Hull Dairycoates.
Hull Alexandra Dock 27/9/37.
Hull Dairycoates 11/6/39.

RENUMBERED:
8252 14/4/46.
68252 8/12/50.

CONDEMNED: 15/4/57.
Cut up at Darlington.

239

Darlington 111.

To traffic 5/1890.

REPAIRS:
???. ?/?—?/8/11.**G**.

239 cont./
Dar. 21/6—11/9/24.**G**.
Dar. 28/12/27—23/3/28.**G**.
Dar. 11/5—23/6/31.**G**.
Dar. 13/3—24/4/36.**G**.
GS buffers fitted.
Dar. 11/4—4/5/40.**G**.
Dar. 3—27/11/43.**G**.
Dar. 19/9—15/10/46.**G**.
Ghd. 5/7—11/8/50.**G**.
Ghd. 12/10—7/11/53.**H/I**.
Dar. 31/8/57. *Not repaired.*

BOILERS:
D789.
    D7 *(new)* ?/8/11.
    2409 *(new)* 23/6/31.
    2847 *(ex1690)* 4/5/40.
D1950 *(ex137)* 27/11/43.
    2533 *(ex8296)* 15/10/46.
    2847 *(exJ72 8715)* 11/8/50.
    2847 reno.25686 7/11/53.

SHEDS:
Hull Alexandra Dock.
Hull Dairycoates 11/9/39.
York 15/1/42
Normanton 9/12/56.
York ?/1/57.

RENUMBERED:
 8253 5/5/46.
68253 11/8/50.

CONDEMNED: 16/9/57.
Cut up at Darlington.

___

50

Darlington 113.

To traffic 6/1890.

REPAIRS:
???. ?/?—?/6/11.**G**.
???. ?/?—?/8/21.**?**.
Dar. 12/1—30/3/27.**G**.
Dar. 8/5—29/6/31.**G**.
Dar. 8/6—5/7/37.**G**.
Dar. 17/8—17/9/42.**G**.
Dar. 4/3—3/4/47.**G**.
Ghd. 25/9—13/10/51.**G**.
Ghd. 26/3—27/4/56.**H/I**.

BOILERS:
D791.
    D3 *(new)* ?/6/11.
    2407 *(new)* 29/6/31.
    AW74 *(ex8261)* 3/4/47.
    25716 *(new)* 13/10/51.

SHEDS:
Shildon.
West Auckland 8/7/35.

RENUMBERED:
 8254 23/6/46.
68254 13/10/51.

CONDEMNED: 7/11/60.
Into Dar. for cut up 8/11/60.

___

241

Darlington 114.

To traffic 6/1890.

REPAIRS:
???. ?/?—?/6/10.**G**.
???. ?/?—?/5/21.**?**.
Dar. 10/9/26—7/1/27.**G**.
Dar. 25/4—31/5/29.**G**.
Dar. 20/7—31/8/34.**G**.
Dar. 11/12/39—9/1/40.**G**.
Dar. 7/3—7/4/45.**G**.
Dar. 28/12/48—15/1/49.**G**.
Ghd. 13/8/52. *Not repaired.*

BOILERS:
D792.
D2058 *(new)* ?/6/10.
    8108 *(new)* 31/5/29.
D1731 *(ex103)* 9/1/40.
    HL90 *(ex260)* 7/4/45.
    2837 *(exJ72 8686)* 15/1/49.

SHEDS:
Shildon.
West Auckland 8/7/35.

RENUMBERED:
 8255 14/4/46.
68255 15/1/49.

CONDEMNED: 18/8/52.
Cut up at Darlington.

___

244

Darlington 115.

To traffic 6/1890.

REPAIRS:
???. ?/?—?/2/08.**G**.
???. ?/?—?/12/21.**G**.
Ghd. 23/2—20/5/26.**G**.
Ghd. 1/6—6/10/27.**H**.
Ghd. 11/12/30—22/1/31.**G**.
Dar. 4/4—5/5/33.**L**.
After collision.
Dar. 6/8—24/9/34.**G**.
Dar. 21/4—1/6/38.**G**.
Dar. 25/8—25/9/40.**G**.
Dar. 20/3—15/4/43.**G**.
Dar. 5—28/9/45.**G**.
Dar. 20/5—11/6/48.**G**.

Ghd. 10/7—18/8/51.**H/I**.

BOILERS:
D793.
D1946 ?/2/08.
D2001 *(new)* 6/10/27.
D1947 *(exJ72 1763)* 25/9/40.
    4585 *(ex252)* 28/9/45.
    3884 *(new)* 11/6/48.
    3884 reno.25607 18/8/51.

SHEDS:
Blaydon.
Heaton 28/7/46.

RENUMBERED:
 8256 25/8/46.
68256 11/6/48.

CONDEMNED: 17/7/54.
Cut up at Darlington.

___

254

Darlington 116.

To traffic 6/1890.

REPAIRS:
???. ?/?—?/6/06.**G**.
Ghd. ?/?—12/5/22.**G**.
Ghd. 11/1—11/3/27.**G**.
Ghd. 27/3—8/5/30.**G**.
???. 22/8—3/9/30.**N/C**.
Vacuum ejector fitted.
Dar. 29 —31/7/31.**N/C**.
Steam heat fitted at front end.
Ghd. 17/3—4/4/32.**N/C**.
GS buffers & hook fitted.
Dar. 19/3—14/4/34.**G**.
Dar. 9/12/36—23/1/47.**G**.
Dar. 17/1—20/2/40.**G**.
Dar. 23/5—25/6/42.**G**.
Dar. 3—30/10/44.**G**.
Dar. 19/3/47. *Not repaired.*

BOILERS:
D794.
D1855 ?/6/06.
D1322 *(new)* 12/5/22.
    8091 *(ex449)* 14/4/34.
    8108 *(ex241)* 20/2/40.
    3267 *(exJ72 2332)* 30/10/44.

SHEDS:
Borough Gardens.
Gateshead 29/5/33.
Blaydon 13/12/37.

RENUMBERED:
 8257 18/8/46.

CONDEMNED: 3/5/47.
Cut up at Darlington.

___

260

Darlington 117.

To traffic 7/1890.

REPAIRS:
???. ?/?—?/3/09.**G**.
Ghd. ?/?—14/12/22.**G**.
Dar. 27/5—30/9/27.**G**.
Ghd. 26/3—1/5/31.**G**.
Dar. 17/6—19/7/36.**G**.
Dar. 19/8—20/9/40.**G**.
Dar. 16/1—8/2/45.**G**.
Dar. 5—19/9/47.**L**.
After collision.
Dar. 13/2—11/3/48.**G**.
Ghd. 17/4—5/5/51.**H/I**.
Ghd. 7—9/5/51.**N/C**.

BOILERS:
D795.
D1992 ?/3/09.
D1999 *(new)* 30/9/27.
    HL90 *(ex482)* 20/9/40.
D2035 *(exJ72 2324)* 8/2/45.
    AW61 *(exJ72 8674)* 11/3/48.
    AW61 reno.25586 5/5/51.

SHEDS:
East Hartlepool.
West Hartlepool 17/4/39.

RENUMBERED:
 8258 11/8/46.
ᴇ**8258** 11/3/48.
68258 5/5/51.

CONDEMNED: 9/11/54.
Cut up at Darlington.

___

296

Darlington 118.

To traffic 7/1890.

REPAIRS:
???. ?/?—?/12/99.**L**.
*Westinghouse equipment fitted
for train brake only.*
???. ?/?—?/4/03.**G**.
???. ?/?—?/1/12.**G**.
???. ?/?—?/3/18.**G**.
???. ?/?—?/3/21.**?**.
Dar. 17/7—14/10/24.**G**.
Dar. 17/3—21/5/28.**G**.

BOILERS:
D796.
D1415 ?/4/03.
D1436 ?/1/12.
    D691 *(new)* ?/3/18.

296 cont./
SHEDS:
Selby.
York 14/5/30.

CONDEMNED: 4/8/33.
Cut up at Darlington.

_____

338

Darlington 119.

To traffic 7/1890.

REPAIRS:
???.   ?/?—?/10/05.**G.**
???.   ?/?—?/3/21.**?.**
Ghd. 27/5—1/9/26.**G.**
Ghd. 14/5—18/6/31.**G.**
Dar. 27/3—28/4/37.**G.**
Dar. 10—29/6/40.**G.**
GS buffers & hook fitted.
Dar. 25/6—30/7/43.**G.**
Dar. 19/3—18/4/46.**G.**
Ghd. 22/11—23/12/49.**G.**

BOILERS:
 D797.
D1853 ?/10/05.
 D128 *(exJ72 1715)* 1/9/26.
D1330 *(ex1153)* 29/6/40.
 HL98 *(ex1196)* 30/7/43.
 8110 *(exJ72 2325)* 18/4/46.
D1950 *(exJ72 8726)* 23/12/49.

SHEDS:
Gateshead.
Darlington 11/11/35.

RENUMBERED:
 8259 18/4/46.
68259 23/12/49.

CONDEMNED: 14/9/55.
Cut up at Darlington.

_____

400

Darlington 120.

To traffic 7/1890.

REPAIRS:
???.   ?/?—?/3/11.**G.**
???.   ?/?—?/12/14.**G.**
Ghd. 25/1—11/4/23.**G.**
Ghd. 24/8—29/10/25.**G.**
Ghd. 12/7—12/9/29.**G.**
Dar. 20/12/35—25/1/36.**G.**
Dar. 6—31/8/40.**G.**
GS buffers & hook fitted.
Dar. 1—27/11/43.**G.**
Dar. 16/1—9/2/49.**G.**

Ghd. 28/5—20/6/52.**G.**
Dar. 2—23/1/56.**G.**
Dar. 31/7—8/8/57.**N/C.**
After collision.
Dar. 2/3/60.*Not repaired.*

BOILERS:
 D798.
D1439 ?/3/11.
 D122 *(ex'964A' 966)* ?/12/14.
AW63 [exE21/13]
(exJ72 2325) 25/1/36.
 2534 *(exJ72 2177)* 31/8/40.
 8114 *(ex54)* 27/11/43.
 HL90 *(ex8255)* 9/2/49.
 25635 20/6/52.
 25659 *(exJ72 69020)* 23/1/56.

SHEDS:
Heaton.
Sunderland 31/1/27.
Darlington 27/9/35.
Middlesbrough 28/7/46.
Thornaby 1/6/58.
Stockton 21/12/58.
Thornaby 14/6/59.

RENUMBERED:
 8260 8/12/46.
68260 9/2/49.

CONDEMNED: 7/3/60.
Cut up at Darlington.

_____

54

Darlington 121.

To traffic 9/1890.

REPAIRS:
???.   ?/?—?/8/10.**G.**
???.   ?/?—?/6/20.**?.**
Ghd. 12/8—10/10/24.**G.**
Ghd. 19/9—17/11/27.**G.**
Ghd. 15/8—25/9/30.**G.**
Dar. 22/11/34—3/1/35.**G.**
*Headlight gear repaired &
refitted.*
Dar. 26/2—23/5/40.**G.**
GS buffers & hook fitted.
Dar. 20/11—8/12/41.**L.**
After collision.
Dar. 8/10—3/11/43.**G.**
Dar. 22/2/47. *Not repaired.*

BOILERS:
 D799.
D2064 ?/8/10.
D2016 *(new)* 17/11/27.
 8114 *(ex1140)* 3/1/35.
AW74 *(ex286)* 3/11/43.

SHEDS:
Borough Gardens.
West Hartlepool 10/11/36.
Darlington 7/11/38.

RENUMBERED:
8261 15/9/46.

CONDEMNED: 22/3/47.
Cut up at Darlington.

_____

103

Darlington 122.

To traffic 9/1890.

REPAIRS:
???.   ?/?—?/3/10.**G.**
Ghd. 25/1—11/4/23.**G.**
Ghd. 15/3—17/6/26.**G.**
Ghd. 1—15/2/29.**L.**
Ghd. 11/7—15/8/30.**G.**
Dar. 24/8—18/10/34.**G.**
Dar. 21/11—16/12/39.**G.**
Dar. 4—30/11/42.**G.**
Dar. 23/4—20/6/45.**G.**
Dar. 30/6—16/7/48.**G.**
Ghd. 11/12/50—11/1/51.**L/I.**
Ghd. 15/3—10/4/54.**G.**
Dar. 18/1/60. *Not repaired.*

BOILERS:
 D800.
D2047 ?/3/10.
D1731 *(new)* 17/6/26.
 2535 *(exJ72 2180)* 16/12/39.
 8107 *(exJ72 8706)* 16/7/48.
 8107 reno.25579 11/1/51.
 25712 *(exJ72 68677)* 10/4/54.

SHEDS:
Heaton.
Gateshead 13/12/37.
Heaton 8/10/48.
Tyne Dock 24/2/57.

RENUMBERED:
 8262 14/4/46.
68262 16/7/48.

CONDEMNED: 25/11/60.
Cut up at Darlington.

_____

176

Darlington 123.

To traffic 9/1890.

REPAIRS:
???.   ?/?—?/2/02.**G.**
???.   ?/?—?/9/20.**G.**

Ghd. 4/8—29/9/24.**G.**
Dar. 3/5—10/8/26.**L.**
Ghd. 16/12/27—18/2/28.**G.**
Ghd. 6/11—15/12/30.**G.**
Ghd. 3—13/2/31.**L.**
Dar. 21/8—25/9/35.**G.**
Dar. 12/5—17/6/39.**G.**
Dar. 8/7—20/8/43.**G.**
Dar. 27/6—10/8/46.**G.**
Ghd. 9—31/5/49.**G.**
Ghd. 14/10—11/11/49.**C/L.**
Ghd. 13/4—2/5/53.**G.**
Dar. 2/6/59. *Not repaired.*

BOILERS:
 D801.
D1410 ?/2/02.
D1966 ?/9/20.
D2035 *(new)* 18/2/28.
D1339 *(ex272)* 17/6/39.
AW56 *(ex177)* 20/8/43.
 2543 *(exJ72 2181)* 10/8/46.
 1943 *(ex8246)* 31/5/49.
 25671 2/5/53.

SHEDS:
East Hartlepool.
West Hartlepool 17/4/39.
Heaton 22/8/54.
Gateshead 9/3/58.
Heaton 26/4/59.

RENUMBERED:
 8263 5/1/47.
68263 31/5/49.

CONDEMNED: 8/6/59.
Cut up at Darlington.

_____

177

Darlington 124.

To traffic 9/1890.

REPAIRS:
???.   ?/?—?/5/08.**G.**
Ghd. ?/?—9/2/22.**G.**
Ghd. 8/2—7/6/27.**G.**
Ghd. 20/2—27/3/31.**G.**
Dar. 10/9—14/10/35.**G.**
Dar. 20/3—15/4/40.**G.**
Dar. 10/6—9/7/43.**G.**
Dar. 27/4—22/5/46.**G.**
Dar. 1—23/12/48.**G.**
Ghd. 16/7—24/8/51.**H/I.**
Dar. 29/11—31/12/54.**G.**
Dar. 11/1/60. *Not repaired.*

BOILERS:
 D802.
D1949 ?/5/08.
D1954 *(new)* 7/6/27.
AW56 *(ex972)* 15/4/40.

By Grouping, quite a number had exchanged the outer of the two handles for a brass wheel. Normanton, June 1936.

(below) In the later 1930's, and during the war, non-ferrous metals were in great demand so by 1945 the brass wheels had all been replaced by steel handles. West Hartlepool, August 1939.

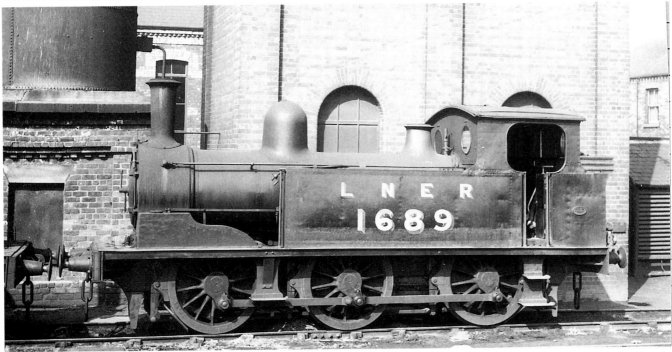

Apart from only two known exceptions, all carried three coal rails which, from 1909, had plating put behind them.

The exceptions were Nos.978 and 286, both of which in LNER days were noted with only two rails.

(below) Both were duly provided with the standard three rails, No.8300 being the 1946 renumber of 978. The illustration at bottom shows No.286 with three rails in September 1938.

Engines shedded at Hull Alexandra Dock shunted the adjacent pit prop and timber storage yards. From 1934 spark arresters with hinged lids were fitted. Alexandra Dock, Hull, September 1938.

177 cont./
4590 *(exJ72 1746)* 9/7/43.
HL98 *(ex338)* 22/5/46.
8100 *(ex8285)* 23/12/48.
8100 reno.25608 24/8/51.
25721 *(new)* 31/12/54.

SHEDS:
Blaydon.
Heaton 17/9/36.
Hull Dairycoates 5/5/57.

RENUMBERED:
8264 24/11/46.
68264 23/12/48.

CONDEMNED: 25/1/60.
Cut up at Darlington.

_____

179

Darlington 125.

To traffic 9/1890.

REPAIRS:
???. ?/?—?/8/09.**G.**
Vacuum ejector fitted 11-12/09.
Ghd. 14/12/22—20/3/23.**G.**
Ghd. 19/2—2/6/26.**G.**
Ghd. 29/10—10/12/28.**G.**
Ghd. 20/2—6/3/30.**L.**
Ghd. 11/9—15/10/31.**G.**
Ghd. 21/12/31—20/1/32.**L.**
GS buffers & hook fitted.
Dar. 25/10—24/11/34.**G.**
Dar. 11/5—24/12/37.**G.**
Dar. 9/7—2/8/40.**G.**
Dar. 27/4—25/5/43.**G.**
Dar. 31/12/45—26/1/46.**G.**
Dar. 5—26/3/49.**G.**
Ghd. 16/8—6/9/51.**H/I.**
Ghd. 20/5—19/6/54.**G.**
Ghd. 21—23/6/54.**N/C.**
Dar. 28/8/59.*Not repaired.*

BOILERS:
D803.
D1995 ?/8/09.
8093 *(new)* 10/12/28.
8111 *(exJ72 1722)* 24/12/37.
D2033 *(ex275)* 2/8/40.
D2010 *(exJ72 2313)* 25/5/43.
D1707 *(exJ72 1747)* 26/1/46.
HL98 *(ex8264)* 26/3/49.
HL98 reno.25589 6/9/51.
25573 *(exJ72 68728)* 19/6/54.

SHEDS:
Borough Gardens.
Gateshead 29/5/33.
Heaton 13/6/48.
Blaydon 14/11/48.
Heaton 20/5/51.

Tyne Dock 4/1/53.

RENUMBERED:
8265 24/11/46.
68265 26/3/49.

CONDEMNED: 31/8/59.
Cut up at Darlington.

_____

181

Darlington 126.

To traffic 9/1890.

REPAIRS:
???. ?/?—?/1/08.**G.**
Ghd. 13/12/24—25/2/25.**G.**
Ghd. 10/8—10/9/26.**L.**
Ghd. 7/6—29/7/30.**G.**
Dar. 5/6—30/7/35.**G.**
New wood buffer beam fitted.
Dar. 22/4—13/5/40.**G.**
Dar. 23/6—6/7/42.**N/C.**
Dar. 28/4—22/5/43.**G.**
Dar. 19/12/45—19/1/46.**G.**
Ghd. 19/10—11/11/49.**G.**
Ghd. 13/7—21/8/53.**L/I.**
Dar. 24/5—1/6/56.**C/L.**
After collision.
Dar. 15/2/57. *Not repaired.*

BOILERS:
D804.
D1945 ?/1/08.
D1728 *(new)* 25/2/25.
8095 *(ex584)* 30/7/35.
2409 *(ex239)* 13/5/40.
7958 *(exJ72 1770)* 22/5/43.
2404 *(exJ72 2317)* 19/1/46.
3896 *(new)* 11/11/49.
3896 reno.25682 21/8/53.

SHEDS:
Blaydon.
Borough Gardens 7/11/31.
Blaydon 26/11/31.
Tyne Dock 22/9/36.

RENUMBERED:
8266 1/12/46.
68266 11/11/49.

CONDEMNED: 18/2/57.
Cut up at Darlington.

_____

248

Darlington 127.

To traffic 9/1890.

REPAIRS:
???. ?/?—?/10/11.**G.**
Ghd. 6/7—8/9/23.**G.**
Ghd. 25/8—1/11/27.**G.**
Ghd. 22/4—23/5/31.**G.**
Dar. 6/3—6/4/35.**G.**
Dar. 4/1—3/2/40.**G.**
Dar. 12/10—10/11/43.**G.**
Dar. 1/7—23/8/47.**G.**
Ghd. 21/8—8/9/50.**G.**
Ghd. 6/7—15/8/53.**L/I.**
Dar. 5/11/57.*Not repaired.*

BOILERS:
D805.
D10 *(new)* ?/10/11.
2403 *(new)* 23/5/31.
7961 *(exJ72 581)* 3/2/40.
4593 *(exJ72 2177)* 10/11/43.
25557 *(new)* 8/9/50.

SHEDS:
Heaton.
Blaydon 1-7/24.
Gateshead 13/12/37.
Heaton 8/10/48.
Blaydon 17/6/51.
Gateshead 13/11/55.

RENUMBERED:
8267 1/12/46.
68267 8/9/50.

CONDEMNED: 25/11/57.
Cut up at Darlington.

_____

478

Darlington 128.

To traffic 10/1890.

REPAIRS:
???. ?/?—?/4/08.**G.**
???. ?/?—23/5/22.**?.**
Ghd. 1/8—6/10/24.**G.**
Ghd. 11/1—16/5/27.**G.**
Ghd. 13/12/29—27/1/30.**G.**

BOILERS:
D806.
D1948 ?/4/08.
D1949 *(new)* 16/5/27.

SHED:
Tyne Dock.

CONDEMNED: 1/9/33.
Cut up at Darlington.

_____

482

Darlington 129.

To traffic 10/1890.

REPAIRS:
???. ?/?—?/11/11.**G.**
Ghd. 8/3—4/5/23.**G.**
Ghd. 10/9—25/11/26.**G.**
Ghd. 29/7—19/9/29.**G.**
Ghd. 5/12/29—17/1/30.**H.**
Ghd. 5—19/9/30.**L.**
Vacuum ejector fitted.
Ghd. 11—22/8/31.**L.**
Ghd. 11/5—17/6/32.**G.**
Dar. 5/6—19/7/35.**G.**
Dar. 2/4—26/5/38.**G.**
Dar. 11/7—7/8/40.**G.**
Dar. 29/9—20/10/42.**G.**
Dar. 4/7—8/8/44.**G.**
Dar. 23/5—15/6/46.**G.**
Ghd. 5/7—19/8/49.**G.**
Dar. 26/5/52. *Not repaired.*

BOILERS:
D807.
D13 *(new)* ?/11/11.
HL890 *(new)* 17/1/30.
HL890 reno.HL90 19/7/35.
2844 *(exJ72 2313)* 7/8/40.
HL96 *(ex572)* 20/10/42.
D2013 *(ex1789)* 8/8/44.
8094 *(exJ72 2315)* 15/6/46.
AW73 *(ex8294)* 19/8/49.

SHEDS:
Borough Gardens.
York 2/7/34.
Selby 13/5/48.

RENUMBERED:
8268 24/11/46.
68268 19/8/49.

CONDEMNED: 26/5/52.
Cut up at Darlington.

_____

802

Darlington 130.

To traffic 10/1890.

REPAIRS:
???. ?/?—?/1/11.**G.**
???. ?/?—?/10/20.**?.**
Dar. 3/5—23/9/26.**G.**
Dar. 22/9—21/10/30.**G.**
Dar. 19/12/35—24/1/36.**G.**
Dar. 3/2—1/3/41.**G.**
Dar. 27/10—24/11/45.**G.**
Ghd. 16/8—15/9/50.**G.**
Ghd. 18—20/9/50.**N/C.**

802 cont./
Ghd. 3/8—17/9/54.**G**.
Dar. 14/10/60. *Not repaired.*

BOILERS:
D808.
D2089 *(new)* ?/1/11.
HL901 *(new)* 21/10/30.
HL901 reno.HL101 24/1/36.
D1999 *(ex1085)* 24/11/45.
25556 *(exJ72 8684)* 15/9/50.
25604 *(ex68240)* 17/9/54.

SHEDS:
Shildon.
West Auckland 8/7/35.

RENUMBERED:
8269 3/11/46.
68269 15/9/50.

CONDEMNED: 14/10/60.
Cut up at Darlington.

_____

77

Darlington 161.

To traffic 11/1891.

REPAIRS:
???.   ?/?—?/1/07.**G**.
???.   ?/?—?/7/09.**G**.
???.   ?/?—?/9/22.**?**.
Ghd. 29/9/26—2/5/27.**G**.
Ghd. 5/1—5/2/31.**G**.
Dar. 16/10—15/11/35.**G**.
Dar. 18/6—8/7/40.**G**.
Dar. 22/8—15/9/44.**G**.
Dar. 14/10—21/11/47.**G**.
Ghd. 23/10—10/11/50.**L/I**.
Ghd. 4—25/2/55.**C/L**.
Dar. 18/11/55. *Not repaired.*

BOILERS:
D934.
D790 ?/1/07.
D1998 ?/7/09.
D1947 *(new)* 2/5/27.
  8100 *(ex495)*15/11/35.
  7954 *(exJ72 2327)* 8/7/40.
  HL96 *(ex482)* 15/9/44.
  AW68 *(exJ72 8736)* 21/11/47.
  AW68 reno.25569 10/11/50.

SHEDS:
East Hartlepool.
West Hartlepool 17/4/39.
West Auckland 27/5/40.
Gorton 30/11/40.
Wrexham 6/12/40.
Bidston 6/12/42.
Wrexham 24/10/43.
Bidston 12/3/44.
York 13/6/44.
Gateshead 31/7/44.

RENUMBERED:
8270 23/6/46.
68270 17/3/50.

CONDEMNED: 21/11/55.
Cut up at Darlington.

_____

161

Darlington 162.

To traffic 11/1891.

REPAIRS:
???.   ?/?—?/12/10.**G**.
Ghd. 2/5—3/7/24.**G**.
Ghd. 24/10—22/12/27.**G**.
Ghd. 9/2—11/3/31.**G**.
Dar. 15/11—19/12/34.**G**.
Dar. 27/9—25/10/38.**G**.

Dar. 23/10—19/11/40.**G**.
Dar. 24/11—10/12/41.**L**.
Dar. 1/6—1/7/43.**G**.
Dar. 4—28/9/45.**G**.
Dar. 18/8—1/10/48.**G**.
Ghd. 2—20/4/51.**H/I**.

BOILERS:
D935.
D2086 ?/12/10.
D2026 *(new)* 22/12/27.
D1952 *(exJ72 1734)* 25/10/38.
HL100 *(ex1833)* 19/11/40.
  2409 *(ex181)* 1/7/43.
AW57 *(exJ72 1734)* 28/9/45.
AW57 reno.25585 20/4/51.

SHEDS:
Blaydon.
Heaton 28/7/46.

RENUMBERED:
8271 8/12/46.
68271 1/10/48.

CONDEMNED: 10/5/54.
Cut up at Darlington.

_____

252

Darlington 163.

To traffic 11/1891.

REPAIRS:
???.   ?/?—?/7/09.**G**.
Ghd. 7/10—8/12/24.**G**.
Ghd. 28/10—29/12/27.**G**.
Ghd. 9/11—11/12/31.**G**.
Dar. 30/7—29/8/35.**G**.
Dar. 18/12/39—12/1/40.**G**.
Dar. 20—27/10/41.**L**.
Dar. 23/10—20/11/42.**G**.

Dar. 1/8—4/9/45.**G**.
Dar. 11—28/9/45.**L**.
Dar. 12/1—20/2/48.**G**.
Ghd. 3—22/12/51.**G**.
Ghd. 8/2—2/3/55.**N/C**.
Ghd. 14/5—8/6/56.**G**.

BOILERS:
D936.
D1993 ?/7/09.
D2015 *(new)* 29/12/27.
D2030 *(exJ72 2333)* 12/1/40.
  4585 *(ex403)* 20/11/42.
  2539 *(exJ72 2313)* 4/9/45.
D1729 *(ex8304)* 20/2/48.
  25614 22/12/51.
  25696 *(exJ72 69025)* 8/6/56.

SHEDS:
Blaydon.
Tyne Dock 22/9/36.
Heaton 4/1/53.
Gateshead 29/11/53.
Thornaby 25/1/59.

RENUMBERED:
8272 1/12/46.
E8272 20/2/48.
68272 22/12/51.

CONDEMNED: 6/2/61.
Cut up at Darlington.

_____

In the later 1940's, twelve J71's, all shedded at West Hartlepool, had internal spark arresters put in for working on their timber docks. No.8305, (ex 1831) was one of those fitted.

25

280

Darlington 164.

To traffic 11/1891.

REPAIRS:
???. ?/?—?/4/05.**G.**
???. ?/?—?/11/21.**G.**
Ghd. 27/7—22/9/27.**G.**
Ghd. 18/12/30—27/1/31.**G.**
Ghd. 22/5—8/7/31.**L.**
Dar. 17/1—15/2/35.**G.**
Sight feed lubricator removed.
Dar. 23/6—29/9/39.**G.**
Dar. 6/7—8/8/42.**G.**
Dar. 1—24/3/45.**G.**
Dar. 9/2—11/3/48.**G.**
Ghd. 11/8—7/9/50.**G.**
Ghd. 29/6—6/8/53.**H/I.**
Ghd. 6—29/6/56.**C/H.**
Dar. 5/11/57. *Not repaired.*

BOILERS:
D937.
D1421 ?/4/05.
D1320 *(new)* ?/11/21.
AW65 [exE21/15]
(exJ72 2327) 15/2/35.
7960 *(exJ72 576)* 29/9/39.
4584 *(exJ72 2311)* 8/8/42.
4077 *(new)* 7/9/50.
4077 reno.25552 7/9/50.

SHEDS:
Heaton.
Blaydon 17/6/51.
York 7/7/57.

RENUMBERED:
8273 15/12/46.
E8273 11/3/48.
68273 7/9/50.

CONDEMNED: 25/11/57.
Cut up at Darlington.

447

Darlington 165.

To traffic 11/1891.

REPAIRS:
???. ?/?—?/11/09.**G.**
Dar. 21/3—31/5/23.**G.**
Dar. 12/8—30/10/25.**G.**
Dar. 15/11/28—3/1/29.**G.**
Dar. 4/11—10/12/31.**G.**

BOILERS:
D938.
D2018 *(new)* ?/11/09.
8088 *(new)* 3/1/29.

SHED:
York.

CONDEMNED: 15/5/37.
Cut up at Darlington.

448

Darlington 166.

To traffic 11/1891.

REPAIRS:
???. ?/?—?/1/10.**G.**
Dar. 27/6—11/9/23.**G.**
Dar. 15/12/25—23/3/26.**G.**
Dar. 25/3—23/5/29.**G.**
Dar. 12/8—13/9/32.**G.**

BOILERS:
D939.
D2020 *(new)* ?/1/10.
8102 *(new)* 23/5/29.

SHED:
Hull Dairycoates.

CONDEMNED: 15/5/37.
Cut up at Darlington.

301

Darlington 171.

To traffic 1/1892.

REPAIRS:
???. ?/?—?/6/12.**G.**
Ghd. 29/1—20/3/24.**G.**
Ghd. 11/2—19/4/28.**G.**
Ghd. 4/2—1/3/29.**L.**
Ghd. 9/12/30—23/1/31.**G.**
Dar. 5/12/34—17/1/35.**G.**
Dar. 20/11—30/12/39.**G.**
Dar. 26/5—17/6/44.**G.**
Dar. 16/5/47. *Not repaired.*

BOILERS:
D944.
D66 *(new)* ?/6/12.
D236 *(ex1758)* 23/1/31.
2539 *(new)* 17/1/35.
2549 *(exJ72 2179)* 30/12/39.
8087 *(ex347)* 17/6/44.

SHEDS:
Borough Gardens.
East Hartlepool 4-7/24.
West Hartlepool 25/3/29.

RENUMBERED:
8274 29/12/46.

CONDEMNED: 14/6/47.
Cut up at Darlington.

449

Darlington 167.

To traffic 1/1892.

REPAIRS:
???. ?/?—?/9/09.**G.**
???. ?/?—?/9/21.**?.**
Dar. 9/2—30/4/25.**G.**
Dar. 16/10—28/11/28.**G.**
Dar. 20/2—17/3/34.**G.**
Dar. 11/10—4/11/39.**G.**
Dar. 6/1—1/2/43.**G.**
Dar. 27/11—29/12/45.**G.**
Dar. 26/11—17/12/48.**G.**
Ghd. 10/6—2/7/52.**H/I.**
Ghd. 14/9—13/10/55.**G.**

BOILERS:
D940.
D2012 *(new)* ?/9/09.
8091 *(new)* 28/11/28.
E21/20 *(exJ72 2332)* 17/3/34.
2533 *(exJ72 2173)* 4/11/39.
AW53 *(ex577)* 1/2/43.
7960 *(ex1123)* 29/12/45.
8090 *(ex8302)* 17/12/48.
8090 reno.25641 2/7/52.
25729 *(new)* 13/10/55.

SHEDS:
Darlington.
Hull Alexandra Dock 29/7/37.
Hull Dairycoates 18/6/39.
York 29/6/40.
Selby 5/2/56.
Normanton 13/9/59.

RENUMBERED:
8275 1/12/46.
68275 17/12/48.

CONDEMNED: 8/2/61.
Cut up at Darlington.

450

Darlington 168.

To traffic 1/1892.

REPAIRS:
???. ?/?—?/7/09.**G.**
Ghd. 12/11/23—30/1/24.**G.**
Ghd. 21/10/26—20/5/27.**G.**
Ghd. 31/12/29—7/2/30.**G.**
Ghd. 26/8—3/10/32.**G.**
Dar. 2/2—3/3/38.**G.**
Dar. 6/6—6/7/42.**G.**

Dar. 2/8—1/9/45.**G.**
Dar. 12/8—3/9/48.**G.**
Ghd. 17/12/51—18/1/52.**H/I.**

BOILERS:
D941.
D1997 ?/7/09.
D1948 *(new)* 20/5/27.
4586 *(exJ72 2174)* 6/7/42.
2882 *(exJ72 2309)* 1/9/45.
2527 *(ex8307)* 3/9/48.
2527 reno.25621 18/1/52.

SHED:
West Hartlepool.

RENUMBERED:
8276 29/12/46.
68276 3/9/48.

CONDEMNED: 19/11/56.
Cut up at Darlington.

451

Darlington 169.

To traffic 1/1892.

REPAIRS:
???. ?/?—?/9/11.**G.**
???. ?/?—?/4/21.**?.**
Hls. ?/?—?/8/24.**G.**
Dar. 28/12/28—21/2/29.**G.**
Dar. 12/10—14/11/32.**G.**

BOILERS:
D942.
D8 *(new)* ?/9/11.
8098 *(new)* 21/2/29.

SHEDS:
Hull Alexandra Dock.
Hull Dairycoates ?/9/25.

CONDEMNED: 15/5/37.
Cut up at Darlington.

452

Darlington 170.

To traffic 1/1892.

REPAIRS:
???. ?/?—?/8/09.**G.**
???. ?/?—?/9/22.**?.**
Dar. 23/10/25—27/1/26.**G.**
Dar. 12/12/28—18/1/29.**G.**
Dar. 30/7—31/8/34.**G.**
Dar. 20/3—8/8/39.**G.**
Dar. 4/11—4/12/41.**G.**
Dar. 10/11—2/12/44.**G.**

Coaching stock shunters in the Newcastle and Gateshead areas were specially fitted with a bracket on the side of the smokebox to carry a lamp, in front of which a red spectacle glass could be displayed. Nos.70, 103, 179, 254, 403, 482, 501 and 1834 were so fitted, some before the Grouping. Gateshead, August 1936.

The spectacle glass was on the end of a rod passing through the boiler handrail and the driver could thus show red or white without leaving the footplate. No.8268 was previously No.482.

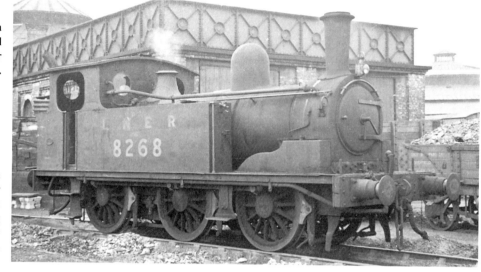

(below) No.70 left the Newcastle area on 5th December 1938, on transfer from Borough Gardens to Darlington shed, but kept its special lamp fitting and still had it for this 11th September 1955 photograph at Darlington works.

By Grouping, eighteen had been fitted for carriage heating with a connecting hose both front and rear. Ten, Nos.54, 70, 179, 254, 403, 482, 501, 811, 1140 and 1834 were all fitted in December 1905. Five were added in 1908-1910. Nos.1134 (February 1908), 399 (March 1908), 1167 (October 1908), 275 (October 1909), 103 (March 1910), followed by 296 (January 1912), and 1197 (October 1914). The NER fitted the last one, No.1163, in June 1922.

The LNER fitted seven more J71, Nos.1690 (January 1928), 493 and 1157 (April 1929), 499 (April 1931), 1831 (June 1932), 1085 (December 1933) and 978 (January 1934). Selby, June 1937.

Although the J71's worked passenger trains when on hire to the Easingwold Railway, none were fitted with other than loose couplings. Easingwold, May 1948.

452 cont./
Dar. 13/2—19/3/48.**G.**

BOILERS:
D943.
D1999 *(new)* ?/8/09.
 8090 *(new)* 18/1/29.
 AW67 *(ex1151)* 4/12/41.
 8108 *(ex254)* 2/12/44.
 7962 *(exJ72 8672)* 19/3/48.

SHEDS:
Darlington.
Hull Alexandra Dock 11/11/31.
Hull Dairycoates 12/6/39.

RENUMBERED:
 8277 5/1/47.
 E8277 19/3/48.

CONDEMNED: 23/11/50.
Cut up at Darlington.

___

401

Darlington 172.

To traffic 1/1892.

REPAIRS:
???. ?/?—?/10/09.**G.**
???. ?/?—?/7/21.**?.**
Ghd. 27/2—29/5/25.**G.**
Ghd. 3/7—17/10/28.**G.**
Dar. 7/9/36. *Not repaired.*

BOILERS:
D945.
D2013 ?/10/09.
 8085 *(new)* 17/10/28.

SHED:
West Hartlepool.

CONDEMNED: 26/9/36.
Cut up at Darlington.

___

572

Darlington 173.

To traffic 2/1892.

REPAIRS:
???. ?/?—?/3/13.**G.**
Ghd. 8/3—14/5/23.**G.**
Ghd. 29/12/26—8/3/27.**G.**
Ghd. 22/4—29/5/30.**G.**
Dar. 19/3—25/4/35.**G.**
GS buffers & hook fitted.
Dar. 22/11—21/12/38.**G.**
Dar. 25/8—24/9/42.**G.**
Dar. 14—24/3/44.**L.**

Dar. 24/1—23/2/46.**G.**
Ghd. 21/3—27/4/48.**L.**
After collision.
Ghd. 7/4—11/5/49.**G.**
Ghd. 19—26/6/50.**C/L.**
Ghd. 20/10—14/11/52.**L/I.**
Ghd. 13/2—9/3/56.**G.**

BOILERS:
D946.
 D129 *(new)* ?/3/13.
 HL892 *(new)* 29/5/30.
 HL892 reno.HL92 25/4/35.
 HL96 *(ex978)* 21/12/38.
 2027 *(exJ72 2324)* 24/9/42.
 AW53 *(ex449)* 23/2/46.
 8114 *(ex8260)* 11/5/49.
 8114 reno.25655 14/11/52.
 25737 *(new)* 9/3/56.

SHEDS:
Heaton.
Blaydon 17/11/51.
Hexham 2/11/52.
Blaydon 2/5/54.
Heaton 22/8/54.
Borough Gardens 2/12/56.
Thornaby 14/6/59.

RENUMBERED:
 8278 5/1/47.
 68278 27/4/48.

CONDEMNED: 6/2/61.
Cut up at Darlington.

___

577

Darlington 174.

To traffic 2/1892.

REPAIRS:
???. ?/?—?/1/04.**G.**
???. ?/?—?/11/19.**G.**
Dar. 8/1—20/3/23.**G.**
Dar. 16/8—22/10/27.**G.**
Ghd. 8/12/31—18/1/32.**G.**
Dar. 13/4—18/5/35.**G.**
Dar. 19/6—9/9/39.**G.**
GS buffers & hook fitted.
Dar. 17/12/42—12/1/43.**G.**
Dar. 17/4—11/5/46.**G.**
Ghd. 7—24/3/51.**G.**
Ghd. 27—30/3/51.**N/C.**

BOILERS:
D947.
D1419 ?/1/04.
 D984 *(new)* ?/11/19.
 4585 *(exJ72 1744)* 18/5/35.
 AW53 *(exJ72 2329)* 9/9/39.
 AW63 *(exJ72 2178)* 12/1/43.
 D1959 *(ex980)* 11/5/46.

25575 24/3/51.

SHED:
Darlington.

RENUMBERED:
 8279 8/12/46.
 68279 24/3/51.

CONDEMNED: 18/6/57.
Cut up at Darlington.

___

1085

Darlington 175.

To traffic 2/1892.

REPAIRS:
???. ?/?—?/10/11.**G.**
Dar. 13/10—13/12/23.**G.**
Dar. 17/8—17/12/26.**G.**
Dar. 7/4—30/5/30.**G.**
Dar. 31/10—1/12/33.**G.**
Vacuum ejector, GS buffers, & screw couplings fitted.
Dar. 25/3—1/5/36.**G.**
Dar. 12/6—8/7/39.**G.**
Dar. 10—17/7/39.**N/C.**
Dar. 23/1—6/3/41.**G.**
Dar. 1/7—12/8/43.**G.**
Dar. 18/7—8/8/45.**L.**
Dar. 17/10—10/11/45.**G.**
Dar. 13/2—18/3/48.**G.**
Ghd. 18/1—10/2/50.**G.**
Ghd. 6/10—1/11/52.**L/I.**
Ghd. 20/7—2/9/55.**G.**

BOILERS:
D948.
 D9 *(new)* ?/10/11.
 HL894 *(new)* 30/5/30.
 8104 *(ex972)* 1/5/36.
 AW71 *(exJ72 2189)* 8/7/39.
 D1995 *(ex541)* 6/3/41.
 D1999 *(exJ72 2321)* 12/8/43.
 D1947 *(ex244)* 10/11/45.
 2539 *(ex8272)* 18/3/48.
 3267 *(exJ72 8752)* 10/2/50.
 3267 reno.25654 1/11/52.
 25580 *(exJ72 68692)* 2/9/55.

SHEDS:
York.
Normanton 8/12/32.
York 17/5/35.

RENUMBERED:
 8280 24/2/46.
 E8280 18/3/48.
 68280 10/2/50.

CONDEMNED: 2/5/57.
Cut up at Darlington.

___

1103

Darlington 176.

To traffic 2/1892.

REPAIRS:
???. ?/?—?/12/09.**G.**
???. ?/?—?/8/21.**?.**
Dar. 7/9—21/12/25.**G.**
Dar. 27/12/28—7/2/29.**G.**
Dar. 20/2—21/3/34.**G.**
New front wood buffer beam fitted.
Dar. 25/3—28/4/38.**G.**
GS buffers & hook fitted.
Dar. 28/12/42—20/1/43.**G.**
Dar. 6—30/3/46.**G.**
Ghd. 22/6—12/7/50.**G.**
Dar. 21/11/53. *Not repaired.*

BOILERS:
D949.
D2017 *(new)* ?/12/09.
 8092 *(new)* 7/2/29.
 8100 *(exJ72 2330)* 20/1/43.
 2010 *(ex179)* 30/3/46.
 HL100 *(exJ72 8742)* 12/7/50.

SHEDS:
Darlington.
Darlington North Road 9/5/38.
West Hartlepool 9/9/51.
Hull Dairycoates 7/6/53.

RENUMBERED:
 8281 3/2/46.
 68281 12/7/50.

CONDEMNED: 23/11/53.
Cut up at Darlington.

___

1140

Darlington 177.

To traffic 3/1892.

REPAIRS:
???. ?/?—?/9/10.**G.**
Vacuum ejector & Westinghouse brake equipment fitted.
Dar. 3/9—15/11/23.**G.**
Dar. 3/2—28/5/27.**G.**
Dar. 7/8—20/9/29.**G.**
Westinghouse equipment removed. Vacuum ejector retained, steam brake refitted.
Dar. 6/4—12/5/32.**G.**
Dar. 19/11—13/12/34.**G.**
Dar. 2/2—31/3/39.**G.**
Dar. 12/2—7/3/42.**G.**
Dar. 10—31/10/44.**G.**
Dar. 8/11—5/12/47.**G.**

No explanation has been found why Darlington based Nos.263 and 449 - *see also* page 22, bottom illustration - had subsidiary coupling rod splashers, the only two so fitted. It is possible that they may have been involved in trials of grease lubrication to the coupling rods like cetain ex GER 0-6-0Ts.

Ex works 1st December 1933, No.1085 was the first to have curved rain strips on the cab roof, with dispersing plates above the cab entrance for protection against rain. York.

(below) Between December 1946 and November 1947, at least sixteen J71's had their cab roofs strengthened by plating in order to protect against large coal falling from overhead coaling plants.

(above) **Where roof protection plates were put on, two sliding ventilators were provided.**

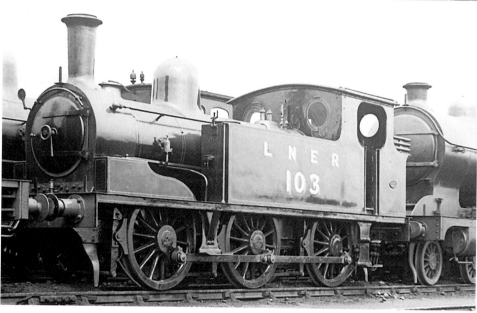

(right) **Normal lubrication was by a cup below the door of the smokebox for the cylinders and an oil box on the front of each tank for the axle journals.**

(below) **In at least a dozen cases, cylinder lubrication was changed to a single sight feed in the cab.**

1140 cont./
Ghd. 16/10—9/11/50.**G**.
Dar. 19/10/53. *Not repaired.*

BOILERS:
D950.
D2066 *(new)* ?/9/10.
  8114 *(new)* 20/9/29.
  8094 *(ex275)* 13/12/34.
  4592 *(exJ72 2187)* 7/3/42.
  2545 *(exJ72 2311)* 31/10/44.
  8111 *(exJ72 8741)* 5/12/47.
  25566 *(ex8308)* 9/11/50.

SHED:
York.

RENUMBERED:
8282 24/2/46.
68282 9/11/50.

CONDEMNED: 26/10/53.
Cut up at Darlington.

_____

1142

Darlington 178.

To traffic 3/1892.

REPAIRS:
???. ?/?—?/8/12.**G**.
???. ?/?—?/10/21.**?**.
Dar. 7/12/25—24/2/26.**G**.
Dar. 16/4—31/5/29.**G**.
Dar. 23/1—16/2/34.**G**.
GS buffers & hook fitted.
Dar. 3/4—12/5/39.**G**.
Dar. 18/3—6/4/40.
Not repaired.
Dar. 7/12/43—1/1/44.**G**.
Dar. 16—23/1/45.**N/C**.
Dar. 10/8/46—15/2/47.**L**.
Dar. 10/8—3/9/48.**G**.
Ghd. 30/6—18/7/52.**H/I**.
Ghd. 13/3—12/4/56.**C/L**.
Dar. 30/7/59. *Not repaired.*

BOILERS:
D951.
  D68 *(new)* ?/8/12.
  8106 *(new)* 31/5/29.
D1993 *(exJ72 2189)* 1/1/44.
HL91 *(exJ72 8677)* 3/9/48.
HL91 reno.25643 18/7/52.

SHEDS:
Percy Main.
Darlington North Road 15/1/23.
Darlington 2-7/46,
Middlesbrough 28/7/46.
Gateshead 5/7/47.

RENUMBERED:
8283 24/2/46.
68283 3/9/48.

CONDEMNED: 30/7/59.
Cut up at Darlington.

_____

1153

Darlington 179.

To traffic 3/1892.

REPAIRS:
???. ?/?—?/9/08.**G**.
???. ?/?—?/3/20.**G**.
Ghd. 29/5—27/7/23.**G**.
Ghd. 4/2—21/3/28.**G**.
Ghd. 18/4—17/5/32.**G**.
Ghd. 1/6—7/7/32.**L**.
Dar. 6/11—13/12/35.**G**.
Dar. 2—26/6/40.**G**.
Dar. 1—15/7/41.**N/C**.
Dar. 21/3—15/4/44.**G**.
Dar. 15/10—9/11/46.**G**.
Ghd. 31/7—25/8/50.**G**.
Ghd. 22/4—7/5/53.**C/L**.
Dar. 6/10/55. *Not repaired.*

BOILERS:
D952.
D1966 ?/9/08.
  D978 *(new)* ?/3/20.
D1330 *(ex453)* 13/12/35.
  HL88 *(exJ72 1746)* 26/6/40.
  4587 *(ex1134)* 15/4/44.
  4581 *(ex8292)* 9/11/46.
  3839 *(exJ72 68687)* 25/8/50.
  3839 reno.25680 7/5/53.

SHEDS:
East Hartlepool.
West Hartlepool 25/3/29.
Darlington 21/1/43.
Blaydon 25/1/43.
Hexham 21/9/47.
Blaydon 2/11/47.
Tweedmouth 13/6/48.
Hull Dairycoates 27/9/53.
Hull Springhead 4/10/53.
Hull Dairycoates 24/1/54.

RENUMBERED:
8284 10/2/46.
68284 22/8/50.

CONDEMNED: 10/10/55.
Cut up at Darlington.

_____

1157

Darlington 180.

To traffic 3/1892.

REPAIRS:
???. ?/?—?/6/11.**G**.
Dar. 24/10/22—19/1/23.**G**.
Dar. 18/4—30/7/25.**G**.
Dar. 17/1—25/3/29.**G**.
Vacuum ejector fitted.
Dar. 6—13/7/32.**N/C**.
Brake connection altered to
swan neck standpipe.
Dar. 19/3—18/4/34.**G**.
Dar. 29/7—1/9/37.**G**.
Dar. 11/7—10/8/40.**G**.
Dar. 19/11—3/12/42.**L**.
Dar. 2—29/12/43.**G**.
Dar. 12/3—6/4/46.**G**.
Dar. 20/9/48. *Not repaired.*

BOILERS:
D953.
  D2 *(new)* ?/6/11.
D2084 *(ex'44' 49)* 30/7/25.
  8099 *(new)* 25/3/29.
E21/19 *(exJ72 2331)* 18/4/34.
D1331 *(ex499)* 1/9/37.
  2534 *(ex400)* 29/12/43.
  8100 *(ex8281)* 6/4/46.

SHEDS:
Normanton.
Selby 5/4/29.

RENUMBERED:
8285 24/2/46.

CONDEMNED: 7/10/48.
Cut up at Darlington.

_____

237

Darlington 181.

To traffic 7/1892.

REPAIRS:
Vacuum ejector fitted 11-12/09.
???. ?/?—?/12/10.**G**.
Dar. 29/9/22—4/1/23.**G**.
Dar. 12/12/24—26/2/25.**G**.
Dar. 22/2—30/4/28.**G**.
Dar. 7/3—10/4/29.**H**.
Dar. 25/2—2/4/31.**G**.
Dar. 18—21/3/32.**N/C**.
Dar. 15/6—14/7/34.**G**.
Dar. 13/5—28/6/35.**H**.
Dar. 23/2—19/3/37.**G**.
Dar. 5/9—6/10/39.**G**.
Dar. 8/12/42—15/1/43.**G**.
Dar. 13/3—13/4/45.**G**.

Dar. 5—31/5/47.**G**.
Ghd. 6/12/49—6/1/50.**G**.
Dar. 16/6/52. *Not repaired.*

BOILERS:
D1015.
D2088 ?/12/10.
  8101 *(new)* 10/4/29.
D1171 *(exJ72 2311)* 28/6/35.
D1322 *(ex493)* 6/10/39.
D2030 *(ex252)* 15/1/43.
D2015 *(ex8242)* 6/1/50.

SHED:
York.

RENUMBERED:
8286 19/5/46.
68286 6/1/50.

CONDEMNED: 16/6/52.
Cut up at Darlington.

_____

240

Darlington 182.

To traffic 7/1892.

REPAIRS:
???. ?/?—?/1/13.**G**.
Ghd. 31/3—28/5/24.**G**.
Ghd. 4/8—26/10/27.**G**.
GS lamp irons fitted.
Ghd. 16/7—21/8/30.**G**.
One new steel & one new wood
bufferbeam fitted.
Dar. 15/11—11/12/34.**G**.
Dar. 17/11/37—6/1/38.**G**.
Dar. 6/1—4/2/42.**G**.
Dar. 2—24/6/44.**G**.
Dar. 19/9/46—15/2/47.**G**.
Ghd. 3—27/1/50.**G**.
Ghd. 1—2/2/50.**N/C**.
Ghd. 20/10—13/11/52.**G**.
Dar. 26/11/56. *Not repaired.*

BOILERS:
D1016.
  D123 *(new)* ?/1/13.
HL897 *(new)* 21/8/30.
HL897 reno.HL97 11/12/34.
  8112 *(ex1199)* 6/1/38.
  2537 *(exJ72 2188)* 4/2/42.
  8112 *(exJ72 2187)* 24/6/44.
  8093 *(exJ72 8694)* 27/1/50.
  25648 13/11/52.

SHEDS:
Tyne Dock.
Borough Gardens 23/10/39.

240 cont./
RENUMBERED:
8287 19/5/46.
68287 27/1/50.

CONDEMNED: 26/11/56.
Cut up at Darlington.

___

402

Darlington 183.

To traffic 7/1892.

REPAIRS:
???. ?/?—?/9/07.**G.**
???. ?/?—?/10/12.**G.**
Ghd. 14/8—8/10/24.**G.**
Ghd. 31/8—3/11/27.**G.**
Ghd. 22/8—1/10/30.**G.**

BOILERS:
D1017.
D1019 ?/9/07.
    D72 (new) ?/10/12.

SHED:
Tyne Dock.

CONDEMNED: 22/9/33.

___

1084

Darlington 184.

To traffic 7/1892.

REPAIRS:
???. ?/?—?/4/10.**G.**
Dar. 16/7—20/10/24.**G.**
Dar. 4/1—28/3/28.**G.**
Dar. 20/1—14/3/31.**G.**
Dar. 2/9—24/10/34.**G.**
Dar. 15/11—11/12/39.**G.**
Dar. 19/6—28/7/43.**G.**
Dar. 8/7—28/8/47.**G.**

BOILERS:
D1018.
D2050 ?/4/10.
D2010 (new) 28/3/28.
D1950 (ex261) 24/10/34.
    8109 (exJ72 2334) 11/12/39.
HL100 (ex161) 28/7/43.
    3280 (exJ72 8720) 28/8/47.

SHEDS:
York.
Hull Alexandra Dock 13/9/37.
Hull Dairycoates 11/6/39.

RENUMBERED:
8288 10/2/46.

___

CONDEMNED: 20/11/50.
Cut up at Darlington.

___

1095

Darlington 185.

To traffic 7/1892.

REPAIRS:
???. ?/?—?/9/06.**G.**
Ghd. 25/9—30/11/23.**G.**
Ghd. 24/5—26/7/27.**G.**
Ghd. 23/4—30/5/30.**G.**
Ghd. 26/10—8/12/32.**G.**
Dar. 31/8—19/10/36.**G.**
Dar. 22/1—19/2/40.**G.**
Dar. 18/12/40—3/1/41.**N/C.**
Dar. 20/9—18/10/43.**G.**
Dar. 16/8—1/9/45.**L.**
Dar. 26/2—27/3/47.**G.**
Ghd. 11/9—4/10/50.**G.**

BOILERS:
D1019.
D1860 ?/9/06.
D1333 (new) 30/11/23.
    D706 (ex326) 8/12/32.
D1333 (exJ72 2323) 19/10/36.
    2523 (ex1689) 18/10/43.
    2537 (exJ72 8721) 27/3/47.
    25560 (ex8269) 4/10/50.

SHEDS:
Tyne Dock.
Borough Gardens 5/2/42.

RENUMBERED:
8289 17/2/46.
68289 4/10/50.

CONDEMNED: 20/6/55.
Cut up at Darlington.

___

1143

Darlington 186.

To traffic 7/1892.

REPAIRS:
???. ?/?—?/2/07.**G.**
???. ?/?—?/4/10.**G.**
Ghd. 3/9—15/11/23.**G.**
Ghd. 26/10—28/12/27.**G.**
Dar. 7/7—3/9/31.**G.**
Dar. 7/7—8/8/36.**G.**
Dar. 14/10—5/11/40.**G.**
Dar. 8—24/2/43.**L.**
Dar. 21/2—16/3/45.**G.**
Dar. 17/2—1/4/48.**G.**
Ghd. 18/6—11/7/51.**H/I.**
Ghd. 22/2—18/3/55.**G.**

___

Dar. 6/1/59. Not repaired.

BOILERS:
D1020.
D1022 ?/2/07.
D2055 ?/4/10.
D2006 (new) 28/12/27.
    HL89 (ex224) 5/11/40.
D2001 (ex224) 16/3/45.
D2001 reno.25601 11/7/51.
    25588 (ex68312) 18/3/55.

SHEDS:
East Hartlepool.
West Hartlepool 17/4/39.
Middlesbrough 25/9/55.
Thornaby 1/6/58.

RENUMBERED:
8290 3/3/46.
68290 1/4/48.

CONDEMNED: 12/1/59.
Cut up at Darlington.

___

1144

Darlington 187.

To traffic 7/1892.

REPAIRS:
???. ?/?—?/6/08.**G.**
Ghd. ?/?—27/10/22.**G.**
Ghd. 18/3—7/7/27.**G.**
Ghd. 11/6—30/7/30.**G.**
Dar. 31/7—12/9/33.**G.**

BOILERS:
D1021.
D1953 ?/6/08.
D1957 (new) 7/7/27.

SHEDS:
Heaton.
Tweedmouth at 12/6/23 (on loan).

WITHDRAWN: 15/5/37.
Sold in June 1938 to Ryhope
Coal Co. Ltd. Scrapped 1/1960.

___

1151

Darlington 188.

To traffic 8/1892.

REPAIRS:
???. ?/?—?/1/07.**G.**
???. ?/?—?/2/16.**G.**
Ghd. 31/10/23—12/1/24.**G.**
Dar. 10/10—23/12/27.**G.**

___

Ghd. 25/8—22/9/31.**G.**
Dar. 6/9—3/11/37.**G.**
Dar. 17/9—18/10/41.**G.**
Dar. 28—30/10/41.**N/C.**
Dar. 6/7—18/8/45.**G.**
Dar. 29/6—6/7/48.**G.**
Ghd. 5—30/11/51.**H/I.**
Dar. 18/4/56. Not repaired.

BOILERS:
D1022.
D1435 ?/1/07.
    D453 (new) ?/2/16.
AW67 (exJ72 2322) 3/11/37.
    8101 (exJ72 2189) 18/10/41.
D1946 (exJ72 2179) 18/8/45.
    2528 (exJ72 8743) 16/7/48.
    2528 reno.25618 30/11/51.

SHED:
West Hartlepool.

RENUMBERED:
8291 10/2/46.
68291 16/7/48.

CONDEMNED: 23/4/56.
Cut up at Darlington.

___

1155

Darlington 189.

To traffic 8/1892.

REPAIRS:
???. ?/?—?/8/10.**G.**
Dar. 9/1—13/3/24.**G.**
Dar. 21/4—30/7/27.**G.**
Dar. 11/2—24/3/31.**G.**
Dar. 14/8—11/10/34.**G.**
Dar. 15/6—24/8/39.**G.**
Dar. 31/8—30/9/43.**G.**
Dar. 17/7—24/8/46.**G.**
Dar. 9/12/48—7/1/49.**L.**
After collision.
Ghd. 20/12/49—20/1/50.**G.**
Dar. 2/10/54. Not repaired.

BOILERS:
D1023.
D2062 (new) ?/8/10.
    2406 (new) 24/3/31.
    4581 (ex1864) 30/9/43.
    2399 (exJ72 8745) 24/8/46.
    2404 (ex8266) 20/1/50.

SHEDS:
Hull Dairycoates.
Selby 18/12/25.
York 20/2/26.
Normanton 12/6/37.

In addition to the cup for cylinder lubrication, Nos.68235 (ex 70) had a ball type fitted on the side of the smokebox. Darlington, May 1951.

Boilers built until about 1928 were fed through clack boxes on the side of the barrel. Springhead, June 1931.

From 1928, boiler feed was through injectors fitted on the face plate. The vacuum ejector exhaust pipe was found to need a drain for the condensate. A small bore pipe emerged from the side of the smokebox and led down through the running plate to discharge on to the track. First fitted was No.499, ex works 2nd March 1937, No.237 getting it on 19th March 1937. York.

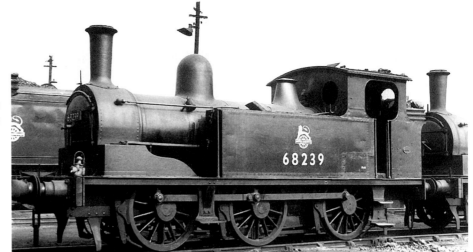

After Nationalisation, at least thirty-nine of the remaining eighty-one changed to under footplate live steam injectors.

Only No.977 was noted as fitted with sliding shutters to reduce the cab side cut-out. This one and No.278 - *see* page 7, 2nd from top - were the only cases which lacked the customary stay to the front footstep. Shildon, May 1932.

(below) Of the five fitted with shunting poles, No.977 seems to have been the only one with brackets at the rear end also. West Auckland, August 1936.

At first the whole class only had steam brake on the engine and ninety-six of them remained that way. In December 1899 No.296 had Westinghouse equipment added for train brakes, the only one to have that combination. It remained so to withdrawal on 4th August 1933. York, June 1932.

In December 1902, No.1197 had its steam brake replaced by Westinghouse gear, for which train connections at both ends were fitted. As late as June 1922 the North Eastern made a similar change to Nos.1163 and 1831, for use on the Selby to Cawood branch.

The three fitted with Westinghouse brakes only lost their purpose when the Cawood branch closed to passengers at the end of 1929. They reverted to steam brake only, No.1163 (July 1929), 1197 (March 1930) and 1831 (November 1937). Darlington Works, August 1935.

In November/December 1909, eight were selected to work as passenger pilots, Nos.237, 399, 1134 and 1167 at York and 179, 501, 811 and 1834 at Newcastle. They remained steam brake only on the engine but had vacuum apparatus fitted for train braking. York, November 1930.

1155 cont./
RENUMBERED:
8292 3/2/46.
68292 7/1/49.

CONDEMNED: 11/10/54.
Cut up at Darlington.

1314

Darlington 190.

To traffic 8/1892.

REPAIRS:
???.   ?/?—?/8/06.**G.**
???.   ?/?—?/4/09.**G.**
Ghd. 3/1—27/3/23.**G.**
Dar. 6/5—24/9/27.**G.**
Dar. 7/7—27/8/31.**G.**

BOILERS:
D1024.
  D531 ?/8/06.
D1994 ?/4/09.
D1993 *(new)* 24/9/27.

SHED:
East Hartlepool.

CONDEMNED: 15/5/37.
Cut up at Darlington.

1196

Darlington 191.

To traffic 11/1892.

REPAIRS:
???.   ?/?—?/5/12.**G.**
Dar. 11/11/24—10/1/25.**G.**
Dar. 12/5—7/8/30.**G.**
Dar. 12—26/11/31.**L.**
Dar. 12/12/35—6/2/36.**G.**
New wood buffer beam fitted.
Dar. 28/10—21/12/39.**G.**
Dar. 20/5—26/6/43.**G.**
Dar. 20/10—17/11/45.**G.**
Ghd. 23/5—23/6/49.**G.**
Ghd. 18/12/52—14/1/53.**L/I.**
Dar. 8/9/56. *Not repaired.*

BOILERS:
D1065.
  D63 *(new)* ?/5/12.
HL898 *(new)* 7/8/30.
HL898 reno.HL98 6/2/36.
  2531 *(exJ72 2184)* 26/6/43.
  8098 *(exJ72 1744)* 17/11/45.
  2543 *(ex8263)* 23/6/49.
  2543 reno.25668 14/1/53.

SHEDS:
Middlesbrough.
York 2/12/33.

RENUMBERED:
8293 26/5/46.
68293 23/6/49.

CONDEMNED: 10/9/56.
Cut up at Darlington.

1197

Darlington 192.

To traffic 11/1892.

REPAIRS:
???.   ?/?—?/12/02.**G.**
Steam brake changed for
Westinghouse brake.
???.   ?/?—?/3/12.**G.**
Dar. 30/7—29/10/25.**G.**
Dar. 17/2—31/3/30.**G.**
Westinghouse equipment
removed & steam brake re-
instated.
Dar. 22/4—7/5/30.**N/C.**
Dar. 10/10—3/11/34.**G.**
Dar. 15/7—23/8/45.**L.**
Brake hangers altered.
Wheels changed.
Dar. 16/11—28/12/39.**G.**
Dar. 27/4—4/6/43.**G.**
Dar. 14/11—13/12/46.**G.**
Ghd. 9/6—1/7/49.**G.**
Ghd. 16/9—9/10/52.**G.**

BOILERS:
D1066.
  D59 *(new)* ?/3/12.
D2091 *(ex978)* 29/10/25.
HL893 *(new)* 31/3/30.
HL893 reno.HL93 3/11/24.
D2004 *(ex261)* 4/6/43.
AW73 *(exJ72 1742)* 13/12/46.
  2406 *(ex8232)* 1/7/49.
  25647 *(exJ72 69002)* 9/10/52.

SHEDS:
Selby.
Normanton 5/4/29.

RENUMBERED:
8294 19/5/46.
68294 1/7/49.

CONDEMNED: 8/11/56.
Cut up at Darlington.

1198

Darlington 193.

To traffic 11/1892.

REPAIRS:
???.   ?/?—?/3/10.**G.**
Dar. 26/4—30/6/23.**G.**
Dar. 24/10—30/12/27.**G.**
Dar. 20/3—8/5/31.**G.**
Dar. 14/9—21/10/38.**G.**
Dar. 16/11—12/12/40.**G.**
GS buffers & hook fitted.
Dar. 13/10—2/11/43.**G.**
Dar. 14/12/45—17/1/46.**G.**
Dar. 27/10—12/11/48.**G.**
Ghd. 2—25/1/52.**G.**
Ghd. 9/1—3/2/56.**H/I.**
Dar. 17/2/59. *Not repaired.*

BOILERS:
D1067.
D2048 ?/3/10.
D2027 *(new)* 30/12/27.
  2872 *(new)* 21/10/38.
D1952 *(ex161)* 12/12/40.
  2528 *(exJ72 1747)* 2/11/43.
  8102 *(exJ72 2321)* 17/1/46.
  2839 *(ex8309)* 12/11/48.
  25610 25/1/52.

SHEDS:
Stockton.
Middlesbrough 5/2/26.
Darlington 18/11/38.
West Hartlepool 2/11/47.
West Auckland 23/6/52.

RENUMBERED:
8295 23/3/46.
68295 12/11/48.

CONDEMNED: 23/2/59.
Cut up at Darlington.

1199

Darlington 194.

To traffic 11/1892.

REPAIRS:
???.   ?/?—?/8/10.**G.**
Dar. 6/10—22/12/23.**G.**
Dar. 8/10/26—25/1/27.**G.**
Dar. 26/4—12/6/29.**G.**
Wheels changed.
Dar. 7/8—15/9/34.**G.**
Dar. 6/10—25/11/37.**G.**
Dar. 10/2—10/3/43.**G.**
Dar. 17/8—14/9/46.**G.**
Ghd. 28/6—5/8/49.**G.**
Ghd. 15/2—11/3/54.**G.**

Dar. 11/7—11/8/56.**C/L.**
Dar. 20/6/58. *Not repaired.*

BOILERS:
D1068.
D2063 *(new)* ?/8/10.
  8112 *(new)* 12/6/29.
D1323 *(ex299)* 25/11/37.
  2533 *(ex449)* 10/3/43.
D1336 *(exJ72 8704)* 14/9/46.
  8098 *(ex8293)* 5/8/49.
  25605 *(ex68298)* 11/3/54.

SHEDS:
Hull Dairycoates.
Hull Alexandra Dock 27/9/37.
Hull Botanic Gardens 11/6/39.
Hull Dairycoates 8/9/49.

RENUMBERED:
8296 23/3/46.
68296 5/8/49.

CONDEMNED: 30/6/58.
Cut up at Darlington.

969

Darlington 197.

To traffic 1/1893.

REPAIRS:
???.   ?/?—?/1/04.**G.**
???.   ?/?—?/7/17.**G.**
Ghd. 16/2—1/5/23.**G.**
Ghd. 24/8—30/10/25.**G.**
Ghd. 21/4—25/6/28.**G.**
Ghd. 30/8—5/9/29.**L.**
Ghd. 19/2—26/3/31.**G.**

BOILERS:
D1071.
D1418 ?/1/04.
  D661 *(new)* ?/7/17.

SHED:
Heaton.

CONDEMNED: 22/9/33.
Cut up at Darlington.

972

Darlington 196.

To traffic 1/1893.

REPAIRS:
???.   ?/?—?/3/10.**G.**
Ghd. 13/11/24—23/1/25.**G.**
Dar. 24/4—13/6/29.**G.**
Vacuum ejector fitted.

972 cont./
Dar. 3—27/5/32.**G.**
Dar. 28/1—27/3/36.**G.**
Standard wheels.
Dar. 3/2—11/3/40.**G.**
Dar. 9/12/43—7/1/44.**G.**
Dar. 11/4—10/5/47.**G.**
Ghd. 25/8—15/9/50.**G.**
Ghd. 2—28/2/53.**G.**

BOILERS:
D1070.
D2052 ?/3/10.
  8104 *(new)* 13/6/29.
  AW56 [exE21/6]
  (ex2189) 27/3/36.
  AW70 [exE21/20]
  (ex449) 11/3/40.
  8106 *(ex1142)* 7/1/44.
  4589 *(exJ72 8739)* 10/5/47.
  25553 *(exJ72 8682)* 15/9/50.
  25644 28/2/53.

SHEDS:
East Hartlepool.
York 28/6/29.
Selby 14/5/30.
York 9/10/34.

RENUMBERED:
  8297 30/6/46.
68297 15/9/50.

CONDEMNED: 21/5/56.
Cut up at Darlington.

137

Darlington 200.

To traffic 1/1893.

REPAIRS:
???. ?/?—?/12/08.**G.**
Ghd. 3/4—12/6/23.**G.**
Dar. 29/8—7/11/27.**G.**
Ghd. 6/3—10/4/31.**G.**
Dar. 12/3—16/4/35.**G.**
Dar. 22/1—1/3/40.**G.**
Dar. 21/10—13/11/41.**N/C.**
Dar. 28/10—20/11/43.**G.**
Dar. 4/12/47—8/1/48.**G.**
Ghd. 4/7—9/8/51.**H/I.**
Ghd. 31/8—25/9/53.**G.**

BOILERS:
D1074.
D1973 ?/12/08.
D2004 *(new)* 7/11/27.
  D981 *(ex533)* 16/4/35.
  D1950 *(ex1084)* 1/3/40.
  D1952 *(ex1198)* 20/11/43.
  HL96 *(ex8270)* 8/1/48.
  HL96 reno.25605 9/8/51.

25674 25/9/53.

SHEDS:
East Hartlepool.
West Hartlepool 17/4/39.
West Auckland 27/5/40.
Selby 10/12/40.
York 28/7/46.
Hull Dairycoates 17/7/49.

RENUMBERED:
  8298 12/10/46.
68298 9/8/51.

CONDEMNED: 27/3/57.
Cut up at Darlington.

977

Darlington 195.

To traffic 1/1893.

REPAIRS:
???. ?/?—?/3/12.**G.**
Ghd. 28/1—26/3/25.**G.**
Dar. 22/4—25/6/30.**G.**
Dar. 22/11—23/12/35.**G.**
Dar. 9/12/40—16/1/41.**G.**
Dar. 16/2—10/3/45.**G.**
Ghd. 14/7—16/9/47.**L.**
Ghd. 13/9—14/10/49.**G.**
Ghd. 24/11/52. *Not repaired.*

BOILERS:
D1069.
  D56 *(new)* ?/3/12.
HL895 *(new)* 25/6/30.
  HL99 *(exJ72 2175)* 16/1/41.
  4005 *(new)* 14/10/49.

SHEDS:
Shildon.
West Auckland 8/7/35.
Borough Gardens 5/12/41.

RENUMBERED:
  8299 25/8/46.
68299 14/10/49.

CONDEMNED: 1/12/52.
Cut up at Gateshead.

978

Darlington 199.

To traffic 1/1893.

REPAIRS:
???. ?/?—?/4/11.**G.**
Dar. 9/1—27/3/23.**G.**
Dar. 27/7—6/10/25.**G.**

Dar. 10/3—19/5/28.**G.**
Dar. 7/7—11/9/30.**G.**
Vacuum ejector fitted.
Dar. 27/12/33—20/1/34.**G.**
Dar. 13—19/4/34.**N/C.**
GS buffers & hook fitted.
Dar. 7/8—9/9/36.**G.**
Dar. 14/10—22/11/38.**G.**
Dar. 5—29/10/40.**G.**
Dar. 2—23/3/43.**G.**
Dar. 7—30/3/45.**G.**
Dar. 3—28/6/47.**G.**
Dar. 7—11/7/47.**N/C.**
Ghd. 30/8—23/9/49.**G.**
Ghd. 30/9—6/10/49.**N/C.**
Ghd. 18/2—8/3/52.**H/I.**
Ghd. 10—13/3/52.**N/C.**
Ghd. 2/6—5/7/54.**C/H.**
Dar. 1/3/55. *Not repaired.*

BOILERS:
D1073.
D2091 ?/4/11.
  D2 *(ex1157)* 6/10/25.
HL896 *(new)* 11/9/30.
HL896 reno.HL96 9/9/36.
  4587 *(ex1835)* 22/11/38.
  HL91 *(exJ72 2178)* 29/10/40.
D1954 *(ex1834)* 23/3/43.
  3508 *(ex8237)* 28/6/47.
  3892 *(new)* 23/9/49.
  3892 reno.25629 8/3/52.

SHED:
Darlington.

RENUMBERED:
  8300 18/8/46.
68300 23/9/49.

CONDEMNED: 7/3/55.
Cut up at Darlington.

980

Darlington 198.

To traffic 1/1893.

REPAIRS:
???. ?/?—?/7/10.**G.**
Ghd. 19/3—4/6/25.**G.**
Ghd. 10/4—27/5/29.**G.**
Dar. 28/8—1/10/34.**G.**
New wood buffer beam fitted.
Dar. 10—20/12/34.**N/C.**
Dar. 5—28/1/39.**G.**
Dar. 3/11—3/12/41.**L.**
After collision.
Dar. 12/10—5/11/43.**G.**
Dar. 23—29/12/43.**N/C.**
*Buffer beam painted with
luminous paint.*
Dar. 31/1—2/3/46.**G.**

Ghd. 7/2—15/4/47.**L.**
After collision.
Dar. 9/2—8/3/49.**G.**
Ghd. 7/4—2/5/52.**G.**
Dar. 26/11/56. *Not repaired.*

BOILERS:
D1072.
D2065 ?/7/10.
  8110 *(new)* 27/5/29.
  2543 *(exJ72 576)* 28/1/39.
D1959 *(ex299)* 5/11/43.
  7958 *(ex181)* 2/3/46.
HL102 *(exJ72 8699)* 8/3/49.
  25625 2/5/52.

SHEDS:
East Hartlepool.
West Hartlepool 17/4/39.
Darlington 1/2/43.
Northallerton 15/4/44.
Darlington 4/5/57.
West Hartlepool 2/11/47.

RENUMBERED:
  8301 12/12/46.
68301 8/3/49.

CONDEMNED: 26/11/56.
Cut up at Darlington.

1666

Darlington 246.

To traffic 11/1894.

REPAIRS:
???. ?/?—?/8/13.**G.**
Dar. 21/2—25/4/23.**G.**
Dar. 10/5—25/6/28.**G.**

BOILERS:
D1187.
  D224 *(new)* ?/8/13.

SHED:
Middlesbrough.

CONDEMNED: 4/8/33.
Cut up at Darlington.

1735

Darlington 247.

To traffic 11/1894.

REPAIRS:
???. ?/?—?/6/10.**G.**
Ghd. 29/7—24/9/24.**G.**
Ghd. 17/2—1/5/28.**G.**
Ghd. 23/5—20/6/29.**L.**

(above) In the early 1900's, No.1140 was changed from steam to Westinghouse and vacuum so as to work as pilot at York carriage works. In September 1929 the Westinghouse was taken off, 1140 then becoming steam and vacuum braked.

During the period 1928 to 1933, ten more steam brake engines had vacuum added for train brakes, Nos.254 (3rd September 1930), 275 (17th July 1930), 403 (19th June 1930) and 482 (19th September 1930) worked at Newcastle; No.978 (11th September 1930) was at Darlington whilst Nos.495 (27th March 1929), 499 (25th April 1931), 972 (13th June 1929), 1085 (1st December 1933) and 1157 (25th March 1929) worked at York or Selby. Newcastle engine No.811 lost its vacuum apparatus on 12th December 1927 when it was put on No.1690 instead on 19th January 1928. York.

Until 1929 the vacuum pipe connection for the train brakes at the front was by a union below the buffer beam. No.1167 was so fitted to 11th June 1929.

On 18th December 1928 an instruction was issued that swan-neck standpipes were to be put on vacuum fitted engines and the eighteen J71's duly got them.

No.978 was ex works 27th March 1923 from a General repair at Darlington and was the first to have the new company initials although the style was still pure North Eastern including the 24in. wide brass number plate. It was the only one so done. No.482 was ex Gateshead on 4th May 1923 and in the new style including standard $8^5/_8$in. wide number plate on the bunker. By the end of June 1923 the first livery change had been made as the full points had been discarded. The 'D' suffix was apparently used on seven of the class: 165, 168, 263, 399, 1085, 1140 and 1758.

(below) From February 1924 until the June 1928 paint economies took effect, standard livery was black with single red lining and one coat of varnish. All 120 had at least one painting in this style.

1735 cont./
Ghd. 17/2—24/3/31.**G**.
Dar. 28/2—6/4/38.**G**.
Dar. 23/9—22/10/40.**L**.
Dar. 19/12/42—14/1/43.**G**.
Dar. 22/8—20/9/45.**G**.
Dar. 10/9—1/10/48.**G**.

BOILERS:
D1188.
D2060 *(new)* ?/6/10.
  2397 *(new)* 24/3/31.
  8097 *(ex1836)* 14/1/43.
  8090 *(ex326)* 20/9/45.
D1731 *(ex8305)* 1/10/48.

SHED:
West Hartlepool.

RENUMBERED:
  8302 3/2/46.
  68302 1/10/48.

CONDEMNED: 30/8/51.
Cut up at Darlington.

_____

1796

Darlington 248.

To traffic 11/1894.

REPAIRS:
???. ?/?—?/9/13.**G**.
Ghd. 12/9—15/11/23.**G**.
Ghd. 30/6—14/10/26.**G**.
Ghd. 9/9—24/10/30.**G**.
Dar. 3/9—2/10/34.**H**.
Dar. 6/11—4/12/39.**G**.
GS buffers & hook fitted.
Dar. 10—29/1/44.**G**.
Dar. 21/1—20/2/48.**G**.
Ghd. 28/10—30/11/49.**C/L**.
After collision.
Ghd. 26/6—14/7/51.**H/I**.
Dar. 19—21/2/53.**C/L**.

BOILERS:
D1189.
  D216 *(new)* ?/9/13.
  2538 *(new)* 2/10/34.
D1331 *(ex1157)* 29/1/44.
AW62 *(exJ72 8691)* 20/2/48.
AW62 reno.25602 14/7/51.

SHEDS:
Borough Gardens.
Darlington 5/11/38.
Middlesbrough 28/7/46.

RENUMBERED:
  8303 24/11/46.
  E8303 20/2/48.
  68303 30/11/49.

CONDEMNED: 13/6/55.
Cut up at Darlington.

_____

1797

Darlington 249.

To traffic 12/1894.

REPAIRS:
???. ?/?—?/7/15.**G**.
Dar. 23/3—27/4/23.**G**.
Dar. 8/10/25—7/1/26.**G**.
Dar. 17/9—15/11/28.**G**.
Dar. 8/6—16/7/31.**G**.
Dar. 20/12/32—13/1/33.**H**.
Dar. 3/8—7/9/34.**G**.
Dar. 12/7—13/8/37.**G**.
Dar. 8/7—8/8/40.**G**.
Dar. 3—25/5/44.**G**.
Dar. 16/12/47—23/1/48.**G**.
Ghd. 18/9—11/10/51.**G**.

BOILERS:
D1190.
  D447 *(new)* ?/7/15.
  2540 *(new)* 7/9/34.
D1949 *(ex1167)* 8/8/40.
D1729 *(ex1833)* 25/5/44.
  3844 *(new)* 23/1/48.
  25715 *(new)* 11/10/51.

SHEDS:
Darlington.
Hull Dairycoates 22/6/39.

RENUMBERED:
  8304 10/11/46.
  E8304 23/1/48.
  68304 11/10/51.

CONDEMNED: 9/11/54.
Cut up at Darlington.

_____

1831

Darlington 250.

To traffic 12/1894.

REPAIRS:
???. ?/?—?/5/12.**G**.
???. ?/?—?/3/22.**?**.
Dar. 8/7—29/12/26.**G**.
Dar. 29/6—6/7/27.**L**.
Ghd. 6/10—11/11/31.**G**.
Dar. 7/10—18/11/37.**G**.
Westinghouse & Heating
apparatus removed. Steam brake
re-instated
Dar. 8/4—3/5/41.**G**.
Dar. 9/4—6/6/45.**G**.
Dar. 1/10—9/11/46.**L**.

Dar. 19/7—26/8/48.**G**.
Ghd. 3—21/9/51.**G**.
Ghd. 7/12/54—7/1/55.**H/I**.
Dar. 14/11/58. *Not repaired.*

BOILERS:
D1191.
  D62 *(new)* ?/5/12.
  4582 *(new)* 11/11/31.
  8113 *(exJ72 2335)* 3/5/41.
D1731 *(ex241)* 6/6/45.
  8113 *(exJ72 8683)* 26/8/48.
  25713 *(new)* 21/9/51.

SHEDS:
York.
Selby 20/2/26.
West Hartlepool 5/4/29.
Stockton 28/7/46.

RENUMBERED:
  8305 31/3/46.
  68305 26/8/48.

CONDEMNED: 24/11/58.
Cut up at Darlington.

_____

1832

Darlington 251.

To traffic 12/1894.

REPAIRS:
???. ?/?—?/1/11.**G**.
???. ?/?—6/4/22.**?**.
Ghd. 8/11/24—7/1/25.**G**.
Ghd. 12/1—16/3/28.**G**.
Ghd. 2/4—13/5/31.**G**.
Dar. 16/8—13/9/35.**G**.
Dar. 28/5—15/6/40.**G**.
Dar. 6—29/6/44.**G**.
Dar. 6—30/8/47.**G**.
Ghd. 8/11—6/12/50.**G**.
Ghd. 22/9—23/10/52.**C/H**.
Ghd. 13/9—14/10/54.**G**.
Dar. 8/7/58. *Not repaired.*

BOILERS:
D1192.
D2087 *(new)* ?/1/11.
  2399 *(new)* 13/5/31.
  2549 *(ex301)* 29/6/44.
  7955 *(exJ72 2308)* 30/8/47.
  4583 *(exJ72 8725)* 6/12/50.
  4583 reno.25651 23/10/52.
  25591 *(exJ72 68672)* 14/10/54.

SHEDS:
West Hartlepool.
East Hartlepool 21/9/36.
West Hartlepool 17/4/39.

RENUMBERED:
  8306 19/5/46.
  68306 6/12/50.

CONDEMNED: 14/7/58.
Cut up at Darlington.

_____

1833

Darlington 252.

To traffic 12/1894.

REPAIRS:
???. ?/?—?/11/12.**G**.
Ghd. 8/11/23—16/1/24.**G**.
Ghd. 15/1—16/4/27.**G**.
Ghd. 26/11/30—6/1/31.**G**.
Dar. 12/4—18/5/35.**G**.
Dar. 16/9—14/10/40.**G**.
GS buffers & hook fitted.
Dar. 5—27/6/42.**N/C**.
Dar. 19/4—8/5/44.**G**.
Dar. 20/5—18/6/48.**G**.
Ghd. 10/9—3/10/51.**H/I**.

BOILERS:
D1193.
  D120 *(new)* ?/11/12.
  HL900 *(new)* 6/1/31.
  HL900 reno.HL100 18/5/35.
D1729 *(ex1688)* 14/10/40.
  2527 *(ex1083)* 8/5/44.
  3885 *(new)* 18/6/48.
  3885 reno.25595 3/10/51.

SHEDS:
Borough Gardens.
Darlington 5/11/38.
Middlesbrough 28/7/46.

RENUMBERED:
  8307 12/5/46.
  68307 18/6/48.

CONDEMNED: 20/6/55.
Cut up at Darlington.

_____

1834

Darlington 253.

To traffic 12/1894.

REPAIRS:
Vacuum ejector fitted 11-12/09.
???. ?/?—?/10/12.**G**.
Ghd. 18/5—31/7/23.**G**.
Ghd. 9/11/25—20/1/26.**G**.
Ghd. 23/7—20/9/28.**G**.
Ghd. 21/5—30/6/31.**G**.
Ghd. 22—25/7/31.**N/C**.
Ghd. 14—22/4/32.**L**.

1834 cont./
Dar. 9/8—22/9/34.**G.**
Dar. 23/2—1/4/37.**G.**
Dar. 18/4—18/5/40.**G.**
Dar. 11/1—6/2/43.**G.**
Dar. 22/8—22/9/45.**H.**
Dar. 18—20/12/46.
Not repaired.
Ghd. 24/12/46—25/1/47.**L.**
After collision.
Dar. 10/1—13/2/48.**G.**
Ghd. 4—29/9/50.**G.**
Ghd. 25/8—12/9/53.**H/I.**
Dar. 15—19/5/58. *Not repaired.*

BOILERS:
D1194.
 D117 *(new)* ?/10/12.
 2404 *(new)* 30/6/31.
D1954 *(ex177)* 18/5/40.
 2397 *(ex1735)* 6/2/43.
 8101 *(ex1151)* 22/9/45.
 HL95 *(ex8247)* 13/2/48.
 4065 *(new)* 29/9/50.
 4065 reno.25558 29/9/50.

SHEDS:
Borough Gardens.
Gateshead 29/5/33.
Heaton 13/12/37.
Darlington 18/8/42.

RENUMBERED:
 8308 12/5/46.
 ᴇ**8308** 13/2/48.
 68308 29/9/50.

CONDEMNED: 19/5/58.
Cut up at Darlington.

1835

Darlington 254.

To traffic 12/1894.

REPAIRS:
???. ?/?—?/1/14.**G.**
Dar. 20/10—20/12/23.**G.**
Dar. 21/1—7/4/27.**G.**
Dar. 14/10—22/11/29.**G.**
Dar. 24/1—18/2/33.**G.**

BOILERS:
D1195.
 D223 *(new)* ?/1/14.
 4587 *(new)* 18/2/33.

SHED:
Neville Hill.

CONDEMNED: 15/5/37.
Cut up at Darlington.

1836

Darlington 255.

To traffic 12/1894.

REPAIRS:
???. ?/?—?/3/11.**G.**
???. ?/?—?/12/20.**?.**
Dar. 4/9—24/11/25.**G.**
Dar. 9/12/30—9/2/31.**G.**
Dar. 4/2—14/3/36.**G.**
Dar. 13/6—5/7/40.**G.**
Dar. 28/11—23/12/42.**G.**
Dar. 20/4—7/6/45.**G.**
Dar. 30/8—24/9/48.**G.**
Ghd. 12/12/51—5/1/52.**L/I.**
Ghd. 3—26/11/54.**G.**
Dar. 2/5/60. *Not repaired.*

BOILERS:
D1196.
D2090 *(new)* ?/3/11.
 2395 *(new)* 9/2/31.
 8097 *(exJ72 1761)* 5/7/40.
AW75 *(exJ72 2182)* 23/12/42.
 2839 *(ex541)* 7/6/45.
 3889 *(new)* 24/9/48.
 3889 reno.25620 5/1/52.
 25651 *(ex68306)* 26/11/54.

SHEDS:
Middlesbrough.
York 2/12/33.
Gateshead 30/6/47.
York 12/4/59.

RENUMBERED:
 8309 19/5/46.
 68309 24/9/48.

CONDEMNED: 9/5/60.
Cut up at Darlington.

1134

Darlington 271.

To traffic 8/1895.

REPAIRS:
Vacuum ejector fitted 11-12/09.
???. ?/?—?/6/11.**G.**
Ghd. 31/7—21/9/23.**G.**
Dar. 24/1—14/4/27.**G.**
Dar. 20/6—16/8/29.**G.**
Dar. 3/5—1/6/32.**G.**
Dar. 26/10—22/11/34.**G.**
Dar. 7/4—7/5/37.**G.**
Dar. 30/10—22/11/40.**G.**
Dar. 16/12/43—8/1/44.**G.**
Dar. 26/10—17/11/45.**G.**
Dar. 19/12/47—30/1/48.**G.**

BOILERS:
D1197.
 D1 *(new)* ?/6/11.
 8113 *(new)* 16/8/29.
AW51 *[exE21/1]*
(exJ72 2313) 22/11/34.
AW60 *(exJ72 524)* 7/5/37.
 4587 *(ex978)* 22/11/40.
AW70 *(ex972)* 8/1/44.
 2397 *(ex1834)* 17/11/45.
 4586 *(ex8251)* 30/1/48.

SHED:
York.

RENUMBERED:
 8310 10/3/46.
 ᴇ**8310** 30/1/48.

CONDEMNED: 6/12/50.
Cut up at Darlington.

1758

Darlington 266.

To traffic 9/1895.

REPAIRS:
???. ?/?—?/7/14.**G.**
Dar. 24/8—26/10/23.**G.**
Dar. 4/1—20/5/27.**G.**
Dar. 21/10—28/11/30.**G.**

BOILERS:
D1198.
 D236 *(new)* ?/7/14.
 D662 *(exJ72 462)* 28/11/30.

SHED:
York.

CONDEMNED: 22/9/33.
Cut up at Darlington.

1789

Darlington 267.

To traffic 9/1895.

REPAIRS:
???. ?/?—?/11/11.**G.**
???. ?/?—?/2/20.**?.**
Dar. 24/8—20/11/25.**G.**
Dar. 24/10—12/12/28.**G.**
Dar. 26/8—29/9/31.**G.**
Dar. 9/8—22/9/34.**G.**
Dar. 22/10—1/12/37.**G.**
Dar. 28/12/39—20/1/40.**G.**
Dar. 23/6—13/7/44.**G.**
Dar. 7/2—11/3/48.**G.**
Dar. 10/8/51. *Not repaired.*

BOILERS:
D1199.
 D12 *(new)* ?/11/11.
 8087 *(new)* 12/12/28.
AW68 *(exJ72 2330)* 1/12/37.
D2013 *(ex268)* 20/1/40.
 4583 *(exJ72 2314)* 13/7/44.
 2524 *(exJ72 8748)* 11/3/48.

SHEDS:
Starbeck.
Hull Dairycoates 12/2/26.

RENUMBERED:
 8311 17/3/46.
 ᴇ**8311** 11/3/48.

CONDEMNED: 10/8/51.
Cut up at Darlington.

1688

Darlington 270.

To traffic 10/1895.

REPAIRS:
???. ?/?—?/1/15.**G.**
Ghd. 6/8—4/11/25.**G.**
Ghd. 29/7—11/9/30.**G.**
Dar. 23/9—20/11/36.**G.**
Dar. 5/8—13/9/40.**G.**
Dar. 21/4—11/5/44.**G.**
Dar. 11/11—11/12/47.**G.**
Ghd. 15/5—8/6/51.**H/I.**
Ghd. 4/1—1/2/52.**C/H.**
Ghd. 11/1—4/2/55.**G.**
Dar. 22/1/59. *Not repaired.*

BOILERS:
D1201.
 D425 *(new)* ?/1/15.
D1729 *(ex242)* 20/11/36.
AW61 *(exJ72 2322)* 13/9/40.
 2542 *(exJ72 571)* 11/5/44.
 3837 *(new)* 11/12/47.
 3837 reno.25588 8/6/51.
 25715 *(ex68304)* 4/2/55.

SHEDS:
Gateshead.
Tyne Dock 29/8/34.
Middlesbrough 18/12/39.
Thornaby 1/6/58.

RENUMBERED:
 8312 19/5/46.
 68312 8/6/51.

CONDEMNED: 2/2/59.
Cut up at Darlington.

After June 1928 unlined black was the rule, even for the Newcastle and York passenger station pilots, through to withdrawal with only one exception.

Ex works 31st May 1947, York station pilot No.8286 (ex 237) came out in fully lined LNER green, even the ends of the front buffer beam having the customary Darlington treatment. The only deviation from pre-war was the change from shaded transfers to cream painted and unshaded letters and numbers in Gill sans style.

Only No.8286 got the green painting and the LNER style lasted until 6th December 1949 when it went to Gateshead for general repair. On 6th January 1950 they turned it out still in green, but now the BR Brunswick variety and although broad black and narrow white lining continued, this was restricted just to a panel on the tank and one on the bunker. On 16th June 1952 it went to Darlington for attention but was withdrawn. York, May 1952.

From July 1942 only NE was used but in 12in. instead of the normal 7½in. size letters. The restoration of LNER in many cases did not occur until after the 1946 re-numbering. No.1735 had 12in. NE when ex works 20th September 1945 and on Sunday 3rd February 1946 West Hartlepool shed changed it to 8302. It remained thus until 1st October 1948.

1689

Darlington 268.

To traffic 10/1895.

REPAIRS:
???. ?/?—?/5/07.**G.**
???. ?/?—?/10/12.**G.**
Ghd. 7/2—2/4/24.**G.**
Ghd. 27/5—26/8/27.**G.**
Ghd. 2/12/30—12/1/31.**G.**
Dar. 17/11—13/12/33.**G.**
Dar. 19/1—14/3/39.**G.**
Dar. 19/8—14/9/43.**G.**
Dar. 6—26/11/48.**G.**
Ghd. 17/3—9/4/52.**G.**
Dar. 31/8/56. *Not repaired.*

BOILERS:
D1202.
D1020 ?/5/07.
  D112 *(new)* ?/10/12.
  2523 *(new)* 13/12/33.
D1330 *(ex338)* 14/9/43.
  2409 *(ex8245)* 26/11/48.
25706 *(new)* 9/4/52.

SHEDS:
West Hartlepool.
West Auckland 27/5/40.
Selby 26/10/40.
York 13/6/48.

RENUMBERED:
  8313 17/3/46.
68313 26/11/48.

CONDEMNED: 3/9/56.
Cut up at Darlington.

1690

Darlington 269.

To traffic 10/1895.

REPAIRS:
???. ?/?—?/7/02.**G.**
???. ?/?—?/11/12.**G.**
Ghd. 15/10—18/12/23.**G.**
Ghd. 15/11/27—19/1/28.**G.**
Vacuum ejector fitted.
Ghd. 4/12/30—19/1/31.**G.**
Ghd. 8—11/3/32.**N/C.**
GS buffers & hook fitted.
Dar. 20/3—17/4/34.**G.**
Dar. 26/11/34—2/1/35.**L.**
After collision.

Dar. 31/8—1/10/37.**G.**
Vacuum drain pipe fitted.
Dar. 3/4—1/5/40.**G.**
Dar. 30/4—23/5/41.**L.**
Dar. 26/11—23/12/42.**G.**
Dar. 7/3—6/4/45.**G.**
Dar. 27/8—27/9/47.**G.**
Ghd. 10/3—8/4/49.**C/L.**
Ghd. 4—28/9/50.**G.**
Ghd. 27/6—22/7/55.**H/I.**
Dar. 2/5/60. *Not repaired.*

BOILERS:
D1200.
D1412 ?/7/02.
  D119 *(new)* ?/11/12.
  D708 *(exJ72 1736)* 17/4/34.
  2847 *(new)* 1/10/37.
  8091 *(ex254)* 1/5/40.
  8088 *(ex495)* 23/12/42.
  8103 *(exJ72 8751)* 27/9/47.
  4066 *(new)* 28/9/50.
  4066 reno.25559 28/9/50.

SHEDS:
Borough Gardens.
Gateshead 29/5/33.
Tweedmouth 17/1/60.

RENUMBERED:
  8314 17/3/46.
68314 28/9/50.

CONDEMNED: 9/5/60.
Cut up at Darlington.

1861

Darlington 272.

To traffic 10/1895.

REPAIRS:
???. ?/?—?/6/02.**G.**
???. ?/?—?/1/14.**G.**
Ghd. 9/2—19/4/23.**G.**
Ghd. 24/11—23/12/24.**L.**
Ghd. 10/9—3/12/26.**G.**
Ghd. 29/5—10/7/31.**G.**
Dar. 18/11—23/12/38.**G.**
Dar. 6/1—1/2/41.**G.**
Dar. 28/9—22/10/43.**G.**
Dar. 14/3/46. *Not repaired.*

BOILERS:
D1203.
D1411 ?/6/02.
  D230 *(new)* ?/1/14.
  D2026 *(ex161)* 23/12/38.

D1707 *(ex70)* 1/2/41.
  2406 *(ex1155)* 22/10/43.

SHED:
Blaydon.

RENUMBERED:
8315 17/3/46.

CONDEMNED: 20/4/46.
Cut up at Darlington.

1862

Darlington 273.

To traffic 10/1895.

REPAIRS:
???. ?/?—?/1/13.**G.**
Ghd. 16—21/2/23.**L.**
Ghd. 10/6—7/8/24.**G.**
Ghd. 9/12/27—15/2/28.**G.**
Ghd. 15/4—18/5/32.**G.**

BOILERS:
D1204.
  D127 *(new)* ?/1/13.
  4588 *(new)* 18/5/32.

SHED:
Borough Gardens.

CONDEMNED: 15/5/37.
Cut up at Darlington.

1863

Darlington 274.

To traffic 11/1895.

REPAIRS:
???. ?/?—?/8/04.**G.**
???. ?/?—?/7/13.**G.**
Ghd. 6/10—6/12/24.**G.**
Ghd. 16/11/28—4/1/29.**G.**
Dar. 12/7—13/8/34.**H.**

BOILERS:
D1205.
  D947 ?/8/04.
  D220 *(new)* ?/7/13.
  2528 *(new)* 13/8/34.

SHEDS:
Sunderland.
Borough Gardens 27/9/35.

CONDEMNED: 15/5/37.
Cut up at Darlington.

1864

Darlington 275.

To traffic 11/1895.

REPAIRS:
???. ?/?—?/5/12.**G.**
Dar. 6/2—10/4/24.**G.**
Dar. 14/1—8/4/27.**G.**
Dar. 15/3—26/4/29.**G.**
Dar. 1—26/2/32.**H.**
Dar. 20/8—6/10/34.**G.**
New wood buffer beam fitted.
Dar. 23/11/39—6/1/40.**G.**
Dar. 17/7—27/8/43.**G.**
Dar. 26/9—23/10/47.**G.**
Ghd. 23/1—16/2/51.**G.**
Ghd. 10/10—4/11/55.**G.**
Dar. 14/10/60. *Not repaired.*

BOILERS:
D1206.
  D64 *(new)* ?/5/12.
  4581 *(new)* 26/2/32.
D1995 *(ex1085)* 27/8/43.
  3275 *(exJ72 8718)* 23/10/47.
  25565 *(ex8297)* 16/2/51.
  25595 *(ex68307)* 4/11/55.

SHEDS:
Hull Dairycoates.
Hull Alexandra Dock 27/9/37.
Hull Dairycoates 12/6/39.
Borough Gardens 1/2/53.
West Hartlepool 14/6/59.

RENUMBERED:
  8316 17/3/46.
68316 16/2/51.

CONDEMNED: 14/10/60.
Cut up at Darlington.

The Darlington works pilot, No.168, had LNER restored when out on 13th April 1946 from a General repair. On Sunday 22nd December 1946 it was renumbered 8236 in painted and unshaded Gill sans making a poor contrast to the LNER in shaded transfers. Not until 7th March 1950 did it have further change. Darlington.

This one had the same style as above but with BR number. Ex Darlington 28th November 1947, it had LNER and 8235 in shaded transfers, but after a collision it went to Gateshead works on 25th February 1948 for a light repair and when out on 6th April 1948 they had applied its BR number but the LNER survived to 4th February 1952.

Between 23rd January and 19th March 1948 no less than fourteen, all at Darlington had BRITISH RAILWAYS and the E prefix to the number put on: E8230 (23rd January), E8244 (6th February), E8247 (12th February), E8249 (11th March), E8258 (11th March), E8272 (20th February), E8273 (11th March), E8277 (19th March), E8280 (18th March), E8303 (20th February), E8304 (23rd January), E8308 (13th February), E8310 (30th January) and E8311 (11th March). West Auckland, March 1951.

The same style and sizes were then used when the 6 superseded the E to show regional ownership. No.68250 was ex works on 30th April 1948.

By 16th July 1948 BRITISH RAILWAYS had been standardised at 10in. and a smokebox number plate was being fitted. No.68256, out 11th June 1948, was the first J71 with a smokebox plate. Note modified 6 both on the plate and on the tank.

From August 1949, BRITISH RAILWAYS was discarded in favour of the emblem but supplies of the transfer for it were slow in reaching Gateshead works, so on 23rd September 1949 No.68300 went back into traffic bearing only the number. Darlington, April 1950. No.68300 returned to Gateshead works a week later for some minor remedial work. The opportunity was taken to apply its missing emblems and it returned to traffic on 6th October 1949.

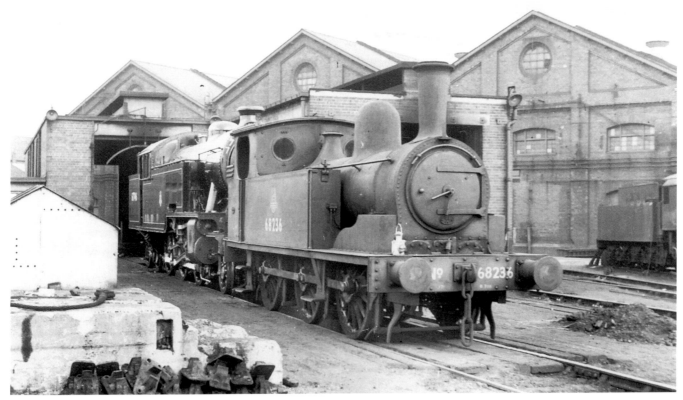

The Darlington works shunter became an oddity. On 3rd February 1950, as LNER 8236, it went to Gateshead works for general repair and when out on 7th March 1950, its smoke box door had been prepared but no plate had been fitted. Instead, its number was on the buffer beam a rare occurrence in combination with the BR emblem. If a plate was cast, this 11th April 1953 photograph shows it had not then been put on and No.68236 was withdrawn on 1st November 1955 without receiving any further repair. Darlington, May 1953.

Otherwise No.68280 shows standard livery for the class from 1949 through to withdrawal because none changed to the BR crest used from 1957.

The last J71 to have a heavy repair was No.68235, ex works 8th February 1957, but fourteen survived into the 1960's, No.68264 being withdrawn on 25th January 1960. Last of class was No.68233, withdrawn 20th February 1961; as No.326, it was built in February 1887 as one of the first ten. Heaton.

When No.304 was withdrawn on 19th February 1936, it was sold to the Cowpen Coal Company where it became Cambois No.12 and survived to 1954 with minimal alterations.

Ten more were built at Darlington during March and April 1899, Nos.1720, 1728, 1733, 1734, 1736, 1741, 1742, 1747, 1749 and 1763, which were similar to the first batch. Note that No.1720, although only steam braked, was used on carriage shunting from its earliest years when it had green paint with lining. No cross handrail was fitted on the back of the bunker.

By Grouping, these twenty were all in black paint and some had their buffers changed from the taper to the parallel shank type. A strengthening stay had been added to the front footstep, and plating fitted to the inside of the coal rails. Heaton, May 1920.

During August to November 1914, Darlington built another twenty, Nos.2173 to 2192 but with modifications made by Raven. The main differences with this batch was that they had a sandwich buffer beam at each end, Ross 'pop' safety valves and a six inches longer bunker. Ten more, Nos.2303 to 2312, were built in 1920.

462

Darlington 351.

To traffic 12/1898.

REPAIRS:
???.   ?/?—?/8/17.**G.**
Dar.   6/10—22/12/23.**G.**
Dar.   25/7—12/10/27.**G.**
Dar.   13/1—18/2/30.**G.**
Dar.   14/11—13/12/32.**G.**
Dar.   17/12/35—10/2/36.**G.**
Spark arrestor fitted.
Dar.   31/10—25/11/39.**G.**
Dar.   4—30/10/40.**G.**
Dar.   10/3—17/4/47.**G.**
Ghd.   11/1—8/2/50.**G**
Ghd.   14/10—1/11/52.**G.**
Ghd.   3/10—1/11/55.**G.**
Dar.   15/1/60. *Not repaired.*

BOILERS:
D1437.
  D662 *(new)* ?/8/17.
  D689 *(ex1746)* 18/2/30.
  D1946 *(ex1763)* 10/2/36.
  HL94 *(ex2332)* 25/11/39.
  2536 *(ex1749)* 30/10/44.
  2523 *(exJ71 8289)* 17/4/47.
  4590 *(ex8690)* 8/2/50.
  25649 1/11/52.
  25750 1/11/55.

SHEDS:
Hull Dairycoates.
Hull Botanic Gardens 1/7/24.
Hull Dairycoates 19/11/29.
Hull Alexandra Dock 12/6/39.
Hull Dairycoates 2/5/54.

RENUMBERED:
  8670 23/6/46.
  68670 8/2/50.

CONDEMNED: 25/1/60 .
Cut up at Darlington.

1715

Darlington 348.

To traffic 12/1898.

REPAIRS:
???.   ?/?—?/4/13.**G.**
Dar.   12/1—29/3/23.**G.**
Dar.   10/2—11/6/26.**G.**
Dar.   4/10—16/11/28.**G.**
Dar.   2/3—7/4/31.**G.**

Dar.   6/5—27/6/32.**H.**
Dar.   14/8—28/9/34.**G.**
New wood front buffer beam fitted.
Dar.   15/12/37—2/2/38.**G.**
Dar.   6/11—3/12/40.**G.**
Dar.   19/4—6/5/44.**G.**
Dar.   18/3—28/5/48.**G.**
Ghd.   14/8—4/9/52.**H/I.**
Ghd.   17/4—17/5/57.**G.**
Dar.   29/2/60. *Not repaired.*

BOILERS:
D1434.
  D128 *(new)* ?/4/13.
  D687 *(ex1744)* 11/6/26.
  D723 *(ex1718)* 28/9/34.
  D1959 *(exJ71 263)* 2/2/38.
  D2006 *(exJ71 1143)* 3/12/40.
  HL97 *(ex1728)* 6/5/44.
  HL97 reno.25646 4/9/52.
  25647 *(exJ71 68294)* 17/5/57.

SHEDS:
Hull Dairycoates.
Hull Alexandra Dock 11/6/39.
York 29/11/41.
Gorton 1/1/42.
Bidston 4/1/42.
Wrexham ?/12/50.
Bidston 1/11/58.

RENUMBERED:
  8671 26/5/46.
  68671 28/5/48.

CONDEMNED: 29/2/60.
Cut up at Darlington.

1718

Darlington 347.

To traffic 12/1898.

REPAIRS:
???.   ?/?—?/5/19.**G.**
Dar.   17/7—20/9/23.**G.**
Dar.   30/6—30/9/26.**G.**
Dar.   5/8—13/9/29.**G.**
Dar.   12/4—8/5/34.**G.**
Dar.   16/3—22/4/39.**G.**
Dar.   13/5—6/6/42.**G.**
Dar.   14/6—13/7/45.**G.**
Dar.   10/2—11/3/48.**G.**
Ghd.   21/8—8/9/51.**H/I.**
Ghd.   24—31/10/51.**C/L.**
Ghd.   26/7—10/9/54.**G.**
Dar.   8/9—9/10/59.**G.**

BOILERS:
D1433.
  D723 *(new)* ?/5/19.
  D1732 *(exJ71 493)* 8/5/34.
  D1151 *(ex1749)* 22/4/39.
  7962 *(exJ71 499)* 6/6/42.
  8092 *(ex8725)* 11/3/48.
  8092 reno.25591 8/9/51.
  25576 *(ex68729)* 10/9/54.
  25692 *(ex68721)* 9/10/59.

SHEDS:
Darlington.
Starbeck 1/7/24.
Neville Hill 1/5/36.
Hull Dairycoates 17/3/57.
Hull Alexandra Dock 21/7/57.
Hull Dairycoates 1/2/59.

RENUMBERED:
  8672 2/6/46.
  ᴇ**8672** 11/3/48.
  68672 8/9/51.

CONDEMNED: 23/10/61.
Into Dar. for cut up 7/2/62.

1721

Darlington 350.

To traffic 12/1898.

REPAIRS:
???.   ?/?—?/7/11.**G.**
Dar.   18/9—22/11/23.**G.**
Dar.   29/6—12/11/26.**G.**
Dar.   4/4—24/5/29.**G.**
Dar.   13/9—25/10/32.**G.**
Dar.   25/3—23/4/37.**G.**
Dar.   28/11—23/12/40.**G.**
Dar.   13/12/44—13/1/45.**G.**
Dar.   2—31/3/48.**G.**
Ghd.   30/10—24/11/51.**G.**
Ghd.   30/6—30/7/54.**G.**
Ghd.   30/10—5/12/58.**G.**

BOILERS:
D1436.
  D4 *(new)* ?/7/11.
  8105 *(new)* 24/5/29.
  2839 *(new)* 23/4/37.
  2872 *(exJ71 1198)* 23/12/40.
  HL94 *(ex462)* 13/1/45.
  D2035 *(exJ71 8258)* 31/3/48.
  25702 *(new)* 24/11/51.
  25748 30/7/54.
  25684 *(ex69004)* 5/12/58.

SHEDS:
Hull Dairycoates.
Hull Alexandra Dock 27/9/37.
Hull Dairycoates 7/11/42.
Hull Alexandra Dock 11/9/49.
Hull Dairycoates 25/2/51.
Hull Alexandra Dock 8/7/51.
Hull Dairycoates 13/11/60.

RENUMBERED:
  8673 20/1/46.
  68673 31/3/48.

CONDEMNED: 8/5/61.
Into Dar. for cut up 9/5/61.

1722

Darlington 354.

To traffic 12/1898.

REPAIRS:
???.   ?/?—?/6/16.**G.**
???.   ?/?—5/5/22.**?.**
Ghd.   4/1—6/2/24.**L.**
Ghd.   26/1—2/4/25.**G.**
Ghd.   10/4—27/5/29.**G.**
Ghd.   11—28/4/30.**L.**
Dar.   15/8—18/9/33.**G.**
Dar.   12/10—17/11/37.**G.**
Dar.   4/12/40—15/1/41.**G.**
Dar.   1—25/5/44.**G.**
Dar.   14/1—7/4/48.**G.**
Ghd.   27/9—19/10/51.**H/I.**
Ghd.   5/3—4/4/56.**G.**
Dar.   2/10—3/11/59.**G.**

BOILERS:
D1440.
  D2049 *(ex '964A' 873)* ?/6/16.
  8111 *(new)* 27/5/29.
  8096 *(exJ71 501)* 17/11/37.
  D1336 *(exJ71 299)* 15/1/41.
  AW61 *(exJ71 1688)* 25/5/44.
  8101 *(exJ71 8308)* 7/4/48.
  8101 reno.25596 19/10/51.
  25704 *(ex68741)* 4/4/56.
  25727 *(ex68726)* 3/11/59.

SHED:
Gateshead.

RENUMBERED:
  8674 20/1/46.
  68674 7/4/48.

CONDEMNED: 16/10/61.
Into Dar. for cut up 26/1/62.

Between April and October 1922 a further twenty-five, Nos.2313 to 2337, were delivered by Armstrong-Whitworth & Co., Newcastle. Like the previous thirty from Darlington, they included a vent pipe on the tank top, a stay to the front footstep, plated coal rails, a horizontal rail across the back of the bunker, and a wheel and handle to fasten the smokebox door. The rectangular markers' plate on the front sandbox was mostly taken off at the change to LNER livery but No.2324 (68731) was still so fitted in June 1950 and No.2327 (68734) still had plates when withdrawn 2nd October 1961.

(below) In November and December 1925, Doncaster built ten J72's, Nos.500, 512, 516, 524, 542, 566, 571, 574, 576 and 581. They were exactly to the Darlington pattern including a forked end to the smokebox door hinge straps.

The basic 1898 design was sufficiently good for British Railways to have Darlington build another twenty engines, Nos.69001 to 69020, from 31st October 1949 to 27th January 1950. Only small detail changes were made; smokebox door fastening was by two handles, the Ross 'pop' valves were enclosed by a Ramsbottom type trumpet, Group Standard buffers and drawhook were fitted, and sanding was steam applied, instead of by gravity, from boxes which included Foreman Downs' patented heating coil to keep the sand dry and free-running. The rear sandboxes were repositioned beneath the bunker. Note the Doncaster style maker's plate. Darlington.

A further eight, Nos.69021 to 69028, were also built by Darlington from 11th April to 12th May 1951. The only difference from the previous twenty was that these eight were fitted with vacuum ejectors for train working but the engine was still steam braked. They also had the Doncaster style elliptical brass plate showing works number and year of building which Darlington began to use in 1943. Unlike the Armstrong-Whitworth plates, Nos.68745 to 68754 and 69001 to 69028 kept their maker's plates until withdrawal.

In 1930 Nos.2184 and 2307, followed in 1942/1943 by 1715 and 2320, were allocated to Bidston, a sub-shed of Wrexham and in 1946 they became Nos.8671, 8701, 8714 and 8727. For working on Birkenhead docks they did not need any alteration. Note No.8671, as one of the first ten built, did not have handrail across the back of the bunker. Heaton Mersey, March 1948.

Ex Darlington 28th May 1948, No.68671 had a shorter cast chimney giving 11ft 0½in. as the maximum height from rail level. This was to enable Wrexham shed to use it in place of J62 class engines on the Connah's Quay-Buckley branch on which there was a low bridge.

1732

Darlington 352.

To traffic 12/1898.

REPAIRS:
???. ?/?—?/5/16.**G.**
Ghd. 9/11/22—2/2/23.**G.**
Ghd. 12/2—9/3/23.**N/C.**
Ghd. 6/8—8/10/25.**G.**
Ghd. 1/2—28/3/28.**G.**
Ghd. 18/7—28/8/30.**G.**
Ghd. 9/11—30/12/32.**G.**
Dar. 3/12/35—24/1/36.**G.**
Dar. 14/9—23/12/37.**H.**
Dar. 22/11—30/12/39.**G.**
Dar. 28/10—26/11/42.**G.**
Dar. 28/6—4/8/45.**G.**
Dar. 24/8—17/9/48.**G.**
Ghd. 22/10—10/11/51.**G.**
Ghd. 10/7—17/8/56.**G.**
Dar. 28/9/61. *Not repaired.*

BOILERS:
D1438.
  D456 *(new)* ?/5/16.
  4594 *(new)* 30/12/32.
  3281 *(new)* 26/11/42.
  D2020 *(ex2305)* 4/8/45.
  HL89 *(ex8712)* 17/9/48.
  25700 *(new)* 10/11/51.
  25738 *(new)* 17/8/56.

SHEDS:
Heaton.
Gateshead 8/10/48.
West Auckland 11/9/60.
Thornaby 19/2/61.

RENUMBERED:
  8675 2/6/46.
  68675 17/9/48.

CONDEMNED: 28/9/61.
Cut up at Darlington.

_____

1744

Darlington 346.

To traffic 12/1898.

REPAIRS:
???. ?/?—?/1/18.**G.**
Dar. 22/9/22—14/2/23.**G.**
Dar. 22/9—11/12/25.**G.**
Dar. 23/8—9/10/28.**G.**
Dar. 1—28/6/32.**G.**
Dar. 19/3—26/4/35.**G.**
Dar. 10/8—9/9/39.**G.**
Dar. 17/12/41—16/1/42.**G.**
Dar. 5—14/12/44.**N/C.**
Dar. 12/9—6/10/45.**G.**

Dar. 27/10—2/12/48.**G.**
Ghd. 5/11—1/12/51.**G.**
Ghd. 30/11—24/12/54.**G.**
Ghd. 20/10—21/11/58.**G.**
Dar. 9/9/60. *Not repaired.*

BOILERS:
D1432.
  D687 *(new)* ?/1/18.
  D59 *(exJ71 1197)* 11/12/25.
  4585 *(new)* 28/6/32.
  AW57 *(ex2319)* 26/4/35.
  8103 *(exJ71 286)* 9/9/39.
  8098 *(ex2181)* 16/1/42.
  AW75 *(exJ71 1836)* 6/10/45.
  8091 *(exJ71 8233)* 2/12/48.
  25692 *(new)* 1/12/51.
  25718 *(new)* 24/12/54.
  25605 *(exJ71 68296)* 21/11/58.

SHEDS:
Darlington *at* 14/2/23.
Hull Dairycoates *by* 6/12/23.
Hull Alexandra Dock 6/4/25.
Hull Dairycoates 7/11/42.
Hull Alexandra Dock 22/5/49.

RENUMBERED:
  8676 12/5/46.
  68676 2/12/48.

CONDEMNED: 9/9/60.
Cut up at Darlington.

_____

1746

Darlington 353.

To traffic 12/1898.

REPAIRS:
???. ?/?—?/11/17.**G.**
Dar. 20/9—27/11/23.**G.**
Dar. 7/2—27/4/27.**G.**
Dar. 16/12/29—31/1/30.**G.**
Dar. 28/10—25/11/32.**G.**
Dar. 24/7—24/8/36.**G.**
Dar. 5/3—2/4/40.**G.**
Dar. 20/5—15/6/43.**G.**
Dar. 26/4—20/6/45.**G.**
Dar. 3/3—30/4/48.**G.**
Vacuum ejector fitted.
Jay-Gee smoke eliminator fitted.
Ghd. 4—28/9/51.**G.**
Smoke eliminator removed.
Ghd. 14/12/53—9/1/54.**G.**
Ghd. 17/9—5/10/56.**H/I.**
Dar. 8/5—26/6/59.**G.**

BOILERS:
D1441.
  D689 *(new)* ?/11/17.
  HL888 *(new)* 31/1/30.
  HL888 reno.HL88 24/8/36.

  4590 *(ex1741)* 2/4/40.
  HL91 *(exJ71 978)* 15/6/43.
  HL94 *(ex1721)* 30/4/48.
  25712 *(new)* 28/9/51.
  25687 9/1/54.
  25713 *(exJ71 68305)* 26/6/59.

SHEDS:
York.
Neville Hill 9/11/49.
York 1/10/50.

RENUMBERED:
  8677 26/5/46.
  68677 30/4/48.

CONDEMNED: 2/10/61.
Into Dar. for cut up 13/12/61.

_____

1761

Darlington 349.

To traffic 12/1898.

REPAIRS:
???. ?/?—?/11/06.**G.**
???. ?/?—?/11/09.**G.**
Dar. 1/5—12/7/23.**G.**
Dar. 15/9/26—21/1/27.**G.**
Dar. 29/12/28—13/2/29.**G.**
Dar. 7/4—28/5/31.**G.**
Dar. 2/8—5/9/34.**G.**
Dar. 29/3—30/4/37.**G.**
Dar. 21/2—15/3/40.**G.**
Dar. 2—29/3/45.**G.**
Dar. 6—29/10/48.**G.**
Vacuum ejector fitted.
Ghd. 21/1—16/2/52.**G.**
Ghd. 19—20/2/52.**N/C.**
Ghd. 14/11—9/12/55.**G.**
Dar. 14—16/12/55.**N/C.**

BOILERS:
D1435.
D1024 ?/11/06.
D2014 *(new)* ?/11/09.
  8097 *(new)* 13/2/29.
D1320 *(exJ71 533)* 15/3/40.
D2020 *(ex8675)* 29/10/48.
  25705 *(new)* 16/2/52.
  25642 *(ex69003)* 9/12/55.

SHEDS:
Darlington.
East Hartlepool 17/11/38.
West Hartlepool 17/4/39.
West Auckland 27/5/40.
Sunderland 31/10/48.

RENUMBERED:
  8678 26/5/46.
  68678 29/10/48.

CONDEMNED: 20/2/61.
Into Dar. for cut up 21/2/61.

_____

1770

Darlington 356.

To traffic 12/1898.

REPAIRS:
???. ?/?—?/12/10.**G.**
Ghd. 5/12/23—12/2/24.**G.**
Ghd. 5/4—19/6/28.**G.**
Dar. 2—22/4/29.**H.**
Ghd. 13/5—17/6/32.**G.**
Dar. 17/9—4/11/36.**G.**
Dar. 3/2—6/3/40.**G.**
Dar. 23/3—19/4/43.**G.**
Dar. 11/3—13/4/46.**G.**
Ghd. 20/4—12/5/50.**G.**
Vacuum ejector fitted.
Ghd. 12—31/1/53.**L/I.**
Ghd. 15/10—9/11/56.**G.**
Dar. 20/6/60. *Not repaired.*

BOILERS:
D1439.
D2085 *(new)* ?/12/10.
  8107 *(new)* 22/4/29.
  7958 *(ex2182)* 6/3/40.
  AW66 *(ex2307)* 19/4/43.
  3272 *(exJ71 499)* 13/4/46.
  4063 *(new)* 12/5/50.
  4063 reno.25673 31/1/53.
  25741 *(new)* 9/11/56.

SHEDS:
East Hartlepool.
Borough Gardens 8/3/37.
Sunderland 28/8/44.
Borough Gardens 6/9/46.
Darlington 11/6/50.

RENUMBERED:
  8679 13/4/46.
  68679 12/5/50.

CONDEMNED: 27/6/60.
Cut up at Darlington.

_____

1720

Darlington 365.

To traffic 3/1899.

REPAIRS:
???. ?/?—?/11/19.**G.**
Dar. 4/6—17/8/23.**G.**
Dar. 5/10/26—26/1/27.**G.**
Dar. 30/7—18/9/29.**G.**
Dar. 3/8—7/9/31.**G.**

1720 cont./
Dar. 8/7—2/9/37.**G.**
Vacuum ejector fitted.Heating apparatus fitted both ends.GS buffers and hook fitted.
Dar. 25/4—18/5/40.**G.**
Dar. 11/12/42—9/1/43.**G.**
Dar. 28/3—21/4/45.**G.**
Dar. 5—24/5/47.**G.**
Dar. 5—29/10/49.**G.**
Ghd. 27/2—14/3/52.**H/I.**
Ghd. 13/10—5/11/54.**G.**
Ghd. 8/7—16/8/57.**G.**
Dar. 10/11—15/12/59.**G.**

BOILERS:
D1442.
D979 *(new)* ?/11/19.
2837 *(new)* 2/9/37.
2404 *(exJ71 1834)* 18/5/40.
8091 *(exJ71 1690)* 9/1/43.
8104 *(ex2329)* 21/4/45.
2536 *(ex8670)* 24/5/47.
2534 *(ex8754)* 29/10/49.
2534 reno.25630 14/3/52.
25556 *(exJ71 68269)* 5/11/54.
25626 *(exJ71 68233)* 16/8/57.
25704 *(ex68674)* 15/12/59.

SHEDS:
Normanton.
York ?/9/25.
Hull Dairycoates 5/11/32.
Gateshead 6/9/37.

RENUMBERED:
8680 7/4/46.
68680 29/10/49.

CONDEMNED: 16/10/61.
Into Dar. for cut up 22/1/62.

1728

Darlington 357.

To traffic 3/1899.

REPAIRS:
???. ?/?—?/5/16.**G.**
Ghd. 1/5—4/7/23.**G.**
Ghd. 24/9—22/12/26.**G.**
Ghd. 17/1—25/2/30.**G.**
Dar. 23/8—6/10/33.**G.**
Dar. 1/2—9/3/37.**G.**
GS buffers & hook fitted.
Dar. 14/5—13/6/41.**G.**
Dar. 25/3—22/4/44.**G.**
Dar. 10/9—17/10/47.**G.**
Dar. 27/10—4/11/47.**N/C.**

Ghd. 28/8—15/9/51.**H/I.**
Ghd. 18—20/9/51.**N/C.**
Dar. 28/9—26/10/55.**G.**

BOILERS:
D1443.
D461 *(new)* ?/5/16.
2536 *(new)* 6/10/33.
HL97 *(ex574)* 13/6/41.
8096 *(exJ71 70)* 22/4/44.
8096 reno.25592 15/9/51.
25733 *(new)* 26/10/55.

SHEDS:
Gateshead.
York 25/8/37.
Neville Hill 28/7/46.
York 27/11/55.
Normanton 4/11/56.

RENUMBERED:
8681 20/1/46.
68681 15/9/51.

CONDEMNED: 22/11/60.
Into Dar. for cut up 24/11/60.

1733

Darlington 358.

To traffic 3/1899.

REPAIRS:
???. ?/?—?/8/15.**G.**
Ghd. 29/10—27/12/23.**G.**
Ghd. 15/6—23/9/26.**G.**
Ghd. 27/12/28—12/2/29.**G.**
Ghd. 2/9—2/10/31.**G.**
Dar. 4—21/4/33.**N/C.**
Dar. 19/2—23/3/35.**G.**
Dar. 14/10—18/11/38.**G.**
Dar. 23/6—29/7/41.**G.**
Dar. 3—10/2/42.**N/C.**
Dar. 1—29/12/43.**G.**
Dar. 23/11—21/12/45.**G.**
Dar. 15—31/1/46.**N/C.**
Dar. 3/2—4/3/48.**G.**
Ghd. 31/7—25/8/50.**G.**
Ghd. 26/1—20/2/53.**G.**
Ghd. 3—27/10/55.**G.**
Dar. 1/12/59. *Not repaired.*

BOILERS:
D1444.
D448 *(new)* ?/8/15.
2527 *(new)* 23/3/35.
D1993 *(exJ71 1314)* 18/11/38.
8110 *(ex1747)* 29/7/41.
2868 *(ex1741)* 29/12/43.

HL101 *(exJ71 802)* 21/12/45.
2872 *(exJ71 8244)* 4/3/48.
8109 *(ex8736)* 25/8/50.
25561 *(exJ71 68250)* 20/2/53.
25732 *(new)* 27/10/55.

SHEDS:
Heaton.
St Margaret's 10/7/24.
Heaton 12/11/24.
Tweedmouth 1/7/56.

RENUMBERED:
8682 2/6/46.
ᴇ8682 4/3/48.
68682 25/8/50.

CONDEMNED: 7/12/59.
Cut up at Darlington.

1734

Darlington 359.

To traffic 3/1899.

REPAIRS:
???. ?/?—?/4/16.**G.**
Ghd. 24/5—27/7/23.**G.**
Ghd. 8/10/26—9/3/27.**G.**
Ghd. 18/10—9/12/29.**G.**
Ghd. 30/5—12/7/32.**G.**
Dar. 20/5—24/6/35.**G.**
Dar. 18/8—13/9/38.**G.**
Dar. 17/12/40—11/1/41.**G.**
Dar. 17/8—10/9/43.**G.**
Dar. 18/7—25/8/45.**G.**
Dar. 27/5—9/7/48.**G.**
Vacuum ejector fitted.
Ghd. 22/10—16/11/51.**H/I.**
Ghd. 2/8—2/9/55.**G.**
Dar. 16/3/61. *Not repaired.*

BOILERS:
D1445.
D455 *(new)* ?/4/16.
D1952 *(exJ71 165)* 24/6/35.
D2032 *(exJ71 168)* 13/9/38.
HL95 *(exJ71 977)* 11/1/41.
AW57 *(exJ71 494)* 10/9/43.
8113 *(exJ71 1831)* 25/8/45.
3887 *(new)* 9/7/48.
3887 reno.25615 16/11/51.
25731 *(new)* 2/9/55.

SHEDS:
Heaton.
West Hartlepool 27/6/48.

RENUMBERED:
8683 12/5/46.
68683 9/7/48.

CONDEMNED: 20/3/61.
Cut up at Darlington.

1736

Darlington 360.

To traffic 3/1899.

REPAIRS:
???. ?/?—?/6/18.**G.**
Dar. 1/5—30/6/23.**G.**
Dar. 24/8—30/10/25.**G.**
Dar. 10/9—26/10/28.**G.**
Dar. 9/6—17/7/31.**G.**
Dar. 13/9—8/12/33.**G.**
Dar. 30/4—31/5/37.**G.**
Dar. 30/4—23/5/40.**G.**
Dar. 25/5—15/6/44.**G.**
Dar. 9/7—6/9/47.**G.**
Ghd. 10/7—18/8/50.**G.**
Ghd. 21—22/8/50.**N/C.**
Ghd. 5—30/10/53.**G.**
Ghd. 2/12/57—3/1/58.**G.**
Dar. 15/3/61.*Not repaired.*

BOILERS:
D1446.
D713 *(new)* ?/6/18.
D708 *(exJ71 399)* 17/7/31.
D1949 *(exJ71 478)* 8/12/33.
8105 *(ex1721)* 31/5/37.
2837 *(ex1720)* 23/5/40.
D1949 *(exJ71 1797)* 15/6/44.
2544 *(ex8731)* 6/9/47.
2545 *(ex68702)* 18/8/50.
25574 *(ex8747)* 30/10/53.
25688 *(ex8745)* 3/1/58.

SHEDS:
Darlington.
East Hartlepool 14/11/38.
West Hartlepool 17/4/39.
Middlesbrough 25/9/55.
Thornaby 1/6/58.

RENUMBERED:
8684 20/1/46.
68684 18/8/50.

CONDEMNED: 15/3/61.
Cut up at Darlington.

WORKS CODES:- Cow - Cowlairs. Dar - Darlington. Don - Doncaster. Ghd - Gateshead. Gor - Gorton. Inv - Inverurie. Kit - Kittybrewster. RSH - Robert, Stephenson & Hawthorn. Str - Stratford. Yk - York.
REPAIR CODES:- **C/H** - Casual Heavy. **C/L** - Casual Light. **G** - General. **H** - Heavy. **H/I** - Heavy Intermediate. **L** - Light. **L/I** - Light Intermediate. **N/C** - Non-Classified.

Darlington supplied the chimneys for the other three J72's for Wrexham shed to fit, which they did in June 1948. No.8701 had LNER restored, ex Darlington 26th June 1947. Wrexham added the 6 to the number on Saturday 25th June 1949 to obviate any confusion with LM Region numbers. Darlington, April 1951.

The four engines with the short chimneys carried them through to withdrawal, all in 1960, No.68701 being the last on 5th October 1960. Note the bunker cross rail on 68727. Bidston, September 1959.

Ex Inverurie works 20th January 1945, No.566 (8750 later) had the chimney off Y9 class No.10094 which then took the J72 chimney. No reason for this solitary exchange has been found, but there was no subsequent reversion.

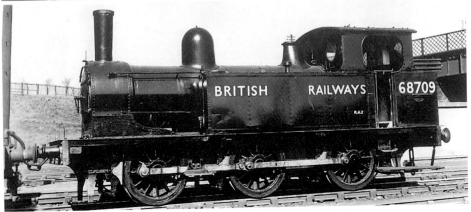

Ex Cowlairs in June 1949, No.68709 was the unfortunate recipient of this stovepipe which it then had to carry until its 26th February 1962 withdrawal.

(above) **Only the twenty built in 1898/1899 had Ramsbottom safety valves fitted when new, but many exchange boilers from J71 class were used by J72 engines and the Ramsbottom valves could be seen on Class J72 to October 1939. They could be identified by the relieving lever across the top of the trumpet shaped casing.**

Ross 'pop' valves superseded the Ramsbottom type and all J72 duly acquired them.

Steam escaping from 'pop' valves tended to obscure the forward view through the cab windows and so it was diverted upwards by enclosing the 'pops' in a Ramsbottom style brass trumpet which then became a standard fitting. Absence of lever across the top indicated 'pop' valves. Sunderland.

1741

Darlington 361.

To traffic 3/1899.

REPAIRS:
???. ?/?—?/4/14.**G.**
Ghd. 27/7—6/9/23.**L.**
Ghd. 4/1—5/3/24.**G.**
Ghd. 29/5—19/7/29.**G.**
Ghd. 7/6—15/7/32.**G.**
Dar. 27/1—20/3/36.**G.**
Dar. 16/12/36—28/1/37.**H.**
Dar. 27/2—19/3/40.**G.**
Dar. 10/11—4/12/43.**G.**
Dar. 7/7—23/8/47.**G.**
Ghd. 1—28/11/50.**G.**
Ghd. 20/6—13/7/51.**C/L.**
Dar. 15—29/9/52.**N/C.**
Ghd. 22/11—17/12/54.**G.**
Dar. 28/9/60. *Not repaired.*

BOILERS:
D1447.
  D233 *(new)* ?/4/14.
  4590 *(new)* 15/7/32.
  2868 *(exJ71 499)* 19/3/40.
  8086 *(ex2186)* 4/12/43.
  8087 *(exJ71 8274)* 23/8/47.
  25568 28/11/50.
  25702 *(ex68673)* 17/12/54.

SHEDS:
Gateshead.
West Hartlepool 12/12/47.
West Auckland 30/4/56.

RENUMBERED:
  8685 17/3/46.
  68685 28/11/50.

CONDEMNED: 3/10/60.
Cut up at Darlington.

1742

Darlington 362.

To traffic 4/1899.

REPAIRS:
???. ?/?—2/5/15.**G.**
???. ?/?—?/10/20.**?.**
Dar. 29/9—17/12/25.**G.**
Dar. 10/5—4/6/29.**N/C.**
Dar. 27/1—6/3/31.**G.**
Dar. 26/6—5/8/36.**G.**
Dar. 15/11—12/12/39.**G.**
Dar. 7/6—16/7/43.**G.**
Dar. 28/9—26/10/46.**G.**
Dar. 4—22/10/48.**G.**
Ghd. 3—20/7/51.**H/I.**
Dar. 31/10—13/12/52.**C/L.**

Ghd. 4—29/10/54.**G.**
Vacuum ejector fitted.
Ghd. 13/8—6/9/57.**G.**
Dar. 14/8/61. *Not repaired.*

BOILERS:
D1448.
  D443 *(new)* ?/5/15.
  2405 *(new)* 6/3/31.
  AW73 *(exJ71 501)* 16/7/43.
  2837 *(ex8705)* 26/10/46.
  2882 *(exJ71 8276)* 22/10/48.
  2882 reno.25606 20/7/51.
  25562 *(exJ71 68234)* 29/10/54.
  25746 *(new)* 6/9/57.

SHEDS:
Stockton.
York 9/10/34.
Normanton 17/5/35.
York 12/6/37.
Hull Alexandra Dock 28/7/37.
Selby 28/5/40.
Hull Alexandra Dock 12/8/40.
York 31/10/54.
Selby 20/4/58.
York 13/9/59.

RENUMBERED:
  8686 17/3/46.
  68686 22/10/48.

CONDEMNED: 14/8/61.
Cut up at Darlington.

1747

Darlington 363.

To traffic 4/1899.

REPAIRS:
???. ?/?—?/9/16.**G.**
???. ?/?—?/11/21.**?.**
Ghd. 19/6—2/10/25.**G.**
Ghd. 13/7—24/10/28.**G.**
Ghd. 18/8—26/9/30.**G.**
Dar. 22/8—29/9/33.**G.**
Dar. 30/7—1/9/36.**G.**
Dar. 21/3—2/5/39.**G.**
Dar. 30/4—26/5/41.**G.**
Dar. 6—30/10/43.**G.**
Dar. 23/11—21/12/45.**G.**
Dar. 6/12/47—2/1/48.**G.**
Vacuum ejector added.
Dar. 26/2—4/3/48.**N/C.**
Steam heating fitted.
Dar. 27/9—6/10/48.**N/C.**
Group Standard buffers fitted.
Ghd. 5/6—4/7/50.**G.**
Ghd. 25/11—20/12/52.**G.**
Ghd. 4/4—11/5/56.**G.**
Ghd. 19/5—20/6/58.**G.**
Dar. 15/9/61. *Not repaired.*

BOILERS:
D1449.
  D2057 *(ex '964A' 967)* ?/9/16.
  8086 *(new)* 24/10/28.
  8110 *(exJ71 980)* 2/5/39.
  2528 *(ex2336)* 26/5/41.
  D1707 *(exJ71 1861)* 30/10/43.
  2531 *(exJ71 1196)* 21/12/45.
  3839 *(new)* 2/1/48.
  8104 *(exJ71 8238)* 4/7/50.
  25656 20/12/52.
  25699 *(ex69021)* 11/5/56.
  25575 *(exJ71 68279)* 20/6/58.

SHEDS:
Heaton.
Blaydon 24/8/52.
Tyne Dock 14/9/52.
York 16/6/57.

RENUMBERED:
  8687 2/6/46.
  ᴇ**8687** 4/3/48.
  68687 6/10/48.

CONDEMNED: 15/9/61.
Cut up at Darlington.

1749

Darlington 364.

To traffic 4/1899.

REPAIRS:
???. ?/?—?/8/13.**G.**
Ghd. ?/?—20/9/22.**G.**
Ghd. 30/4—4/8/25.**G.**
Ghd. 24/3—12/4/26.**L.**
Ghd. 27/9—8/11/28.**G.**
Ghd. 28/7—28/8/31.**G.**
Dar. 5/4—2/5/34.**H.**
Dar. 18/6—13/8/35.**G.**
Dar. 14/3—20/4/39.**G.**
Dar. 7/7—11/8/41.**G.**
Dar. 18—20/12/43.**N/C.**
Luminous paint on buffer beam.
Dar. 20/9—14/10/44.**G.**
Dar. 22/3—4/6/48.**G.**
Ghd. 4—22/9/51.**H/I.**
Dar. 25/3—16/4/55.**G.**
Dar. 18—20/4/55.**N/C.**
Dar. 12/9—13/10/59.**G.**

BOILERS:
D1450.
  D214 *(new)* ?/8/13.
  D1151 *(ex2304)* 2/5/34.
  7959 *(ex2181)* 20/4/39.
  2536 *(ex1728)* 11/8/41.
  3519 *(new)* 14/10/44.
  3519 reno.25593 22/9/51.
  25720 *(new)* 16/4/55.
  25735 *(ex68751)* 13/10/59.

SHEDS:
Heaton.
Darlington 19/5/43.
Middlesbrough 13/6/48.
Thornaby 1/6/58.
West Auckland 9/10/60.
Thornaby 19/2/61.

RENUMBERED:
  8688 2/6/46.
  68688 4/6/48.

CONDEMNED: 16/10/61.
Into Dar. for cut up 4/1/62.

1763

Darlington 355.

To traffic 4/1899.

REPAIRS:
???. ?/?—?/10/10.**G.**
Ghd. ?/?—20/7/22.**G.**
Ghd. 15/9—5/5/27.**G.**
Ghd. 3/3—8/4/31.**G.**
Ghd. 28/10—16/11/32.**L.**
Dar. 2/12/35—10/1/36.**G.**
Dar. 23/7—23/8/40.**G.**
Dar. 21/10—18/11/44.**G.**
Dar. 16/12/47—16/1/48.**G.**
Vacuum ejector fitted.
Dar. 5—9/4/48.**N/C.**
Ghd. 15/10—10/11/51.**H/I.**
Ghd. 23/5—30/6/55.**G.**
Dar. 8/5—19/6/59.**G.**

BOILERS:
D1451.
D2082 ?/10/10.
D1946 *(new)* 5/5/27.
D1947 *(exJ71 77)* 10/1/36.
  2540 *(exJ71 1797)* 23/8/40.
  8085 *(ex524)* 18/11/44.
  3842 *(new)* 16/1/48.
  3842 reno.25598 10/11/51.
  25725 *(new)* 30/6/55.
  25714 *(ex69001)* 19/6/59.

SHEDS:
East Hartlepool.
West Hartlepool 17/4/39.
Middlesbrough 25/7/48.
Thornaby 1/6/58.

RENUMBERED:
  8689 31/3/46.
  68689 9/4/48.

CONDEMNED: 16/10/61.
Into Dar. for cut up 5/1/62.

Before enclosure of the 'pop' valves became official, many crews improvised one, even from empty paint cans.

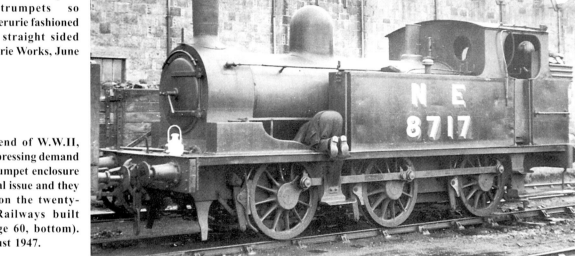

Engines transferred to the Scottish Area and maintained there did not have access to spare Ramsbottom trumpets so Cowlairs and Inverurie fashioned their own deep straight sided enclosure. Inverurie Works, June 1946.

(below) By the end of W.W.II, brass was in less pressing demand and enabled a trumpet enclosure to be made official issue and they were standard on the twenty-eight British Railways built engines (see page 60, bottom). Darlington, August 1947.

(above) **The first twenty engines had a high-pitched bell shape whistle but a December 1909 instruction led to these being changed to a lower toned organ pipe whistle which all later-built engines had from new.**

Odd exceptions crept in of bell shaped whistles being fitted in LNER days but No.2334 was the only one seen in original numbering. In Scotland, Nos.8749 and 8750 were so fitted by 1946. In British Railways livery Nos.68710, 68711, 68741 and 68742 were all seen with these whistles.

No.1746 was the only one seen with this pipe cover to divert steam from the whistle away from the cab windows and it was clearly an unofficial addition.

2173

Darlington.

To traffic 8/1914.

REPAIRS:
???. ?/?—?/10/20.**?**.
???. ?/?—26/7/22.**?**.
Ghd. 29/1—4/4/25.**G**.
Ghd. 31/1—27/3/28.**G**.
Ghd. 28/1—12/3/31.**G**.
Dar. 31/8—16/10/34.**G**.
Dar. 4/9—6/10/39.**G**.
Dar. 26/8—17/9/43.**G**.
Dar. 17—19/1/44.**N/C**.
Luminous paint on buffer beam.
Dar. 14/6—12/7/46.**G**.
Ghd. 13/12/49—20/1/50.**G**.
Ghd. 10/6—2/7/53.**L/I**.
Ghd. 4—21/12/56.**G**.
Vacuum ejector fitted.
Ghd. 7/5—4/6/58.**C/H**.

BOILERS:
D331.
2533 *(new)* 16/10/34.
D1171 *(exJ71 237)* 6/10/39.
D1339 *(exJ71 176)* 17/9/43.
4590 *(exJ71 177)* 12/7/46.
4044 *(new)* 20/1/50.
4044 reno.25681 2/7/53.
25690 *(ex68731)* 21/12/56.

SHEDS:
West Hartlepool.
West Auckland 27/5/40.
Middlesbrough 16/5/41.
Thornaby 1/6/58.

RENUMBERED:
8690 12/7/46.
68690 20/1/50.

CONDEMNED: 20/2/61.
Into Dar. for cut up 21/2/61.

2174

Darlington.

To traffic 9/1914.

REPAIRS:
Ghd. 11/1—3/3/24.**G**.
Dar. 7—25/3/24.**L**.
Ghd. 10/8—11/11/27.**G**.
Ghd. 16/10—12/11/31.**G**.
Dar. 7/10—7/11/35.**G**.
Dar. 24/2—27/6/39.**G**.
Dar. 16/3—13/4/42.**G**.
Dar. 28/9—21/10/44.**G**.
Dar. 26/9/47—16/4/48.**G**.
Ghd. 14/1—6/2/52.**H/I**.

Dar. 2/8—3/9/55.**G**.
Dar. 5—6/9/55.**N/C**.

BOILERS:
D334.
4584 *(new)* 12/11/31.
4586 *(ex2186)* 27/6/39.
AW68 *(ex500)* 13/4/42.
AW62 *(ex2319)* 21/10/44.
D2022 *(ex8727)* 16/4/48.
D2022 reno.25622 6/2/52.
25707 *(ex68735)* 3/9/55.

SHEDS:
West Hartlepool.
Sunderland 31/1/27.
West Auckland 31/10/48.

RENUMBERED:
8691 26/5/46.
68691 16/4/48.

CONDEMNED: 19/12/60.
Into Dar. for cut up 22/12/60.

2175

Darlington.

To traffic 9/1914.

REPAIRS:
Ghd. 5/4—3/6/24.**G**.
Dar. 6/5—11/8/27.**G**.
Ghd. 14/5—24/6/30.**G**.
Dar. 4/8—7/9/33.**G**.
Dar. 3/5—7/6/37.**G**.
Dar. 30/10—22/11/40.**G**.
Dar. 8/2—3/3/45.**G**.
Dar. 27/2—25/3/48.**G**.
Ghd. 9—28/4/51.**G**.
Ghd. 23/6—15/7/55.**G**.

BOILERS:
D336.
HL899 *(new)* 24/6/30.
HL899 reno.HL99 7/6/37.
AW54 *(ex2321)* 22/11/40.
AW67 *(exJ71 452)* 3/3/45.
3281 *(ex8729)* 25/3/48.
25580 28/4/51.
25598 *(ex68689)* 15/7/55.

SHEDS:
West Hartlepool.
West Auckland 8/3/53.

RENUMBERED:
8692 16/6/46.
68692 25/3/48.

CONDEMNED: 2/10/61.
Into Dar. for cut up 19/10/61.

2176

Darlington.

To traffic 9/1914.

REPAIRS:
Ghd. 7/9—7/11/23.**G**.
Dar. 7/3—21/5/27.**G**.
Ghd. 19/11/29—7/1/30.**G**.
Ghd. 3/11—2/12/32.**G**.
Dar. 31/7—4/9/36.**G**.
Dar. 13/7—9/8/40.**G**.
Dar. 4—30/8/44.**G**.
Dar. 18/11—12/12/47.**G**.
Vacuum ejector fitted.
Dar. 9—17/3/48.**N/C**.
Steam heater fitted.
Dar. 6—14/10/48.**N/C**.
Group Standard buffers fitted.
Ghd. 14/6—7/7/50.**G**.
Ghd. 30/3—22/4/53.**H/I**.
Ghd. 5/12/55—6/1/56.**G**.
Ghd. 12/5—6/6/58.**G**.
Dar. 24/8/61. *Not repaired.*

BOILERS:
D339.
4593 *(new)* 2/12/32.
8111 *(exJ71 179)* 9/8/40.
D1728 *(ex2188)* 30/8/44.
4588 *(exJ71 8235)* 12/12/47.
2523 *(ex8670)* 7/7/50.
2523 reno.25679 22/4/53.
25587 *(ex68707)* 6/1/56.
25593 *(ex68737)* 6/6/58.

SHEDS:
West Hartlepool.
Gateshead 12/12/47.

RENUMBERED:
8693 16/6/46.
ᴇ**8693** 17/3/48.
68693 14/10/48.

CONDEMNED: 24/8/61.
Cut up at Darlington.

2177

Darlington.

To traffic 9/1914.

REPAIRS:
Ghd. ?/?—22/9/22.**G**.
Ghd. 27/3—8/7/25.**G**.
Ghd. 18/7—3/9/29.**G**.
Ghd. 2/2—3/3/32.**G**.
Dar. 17/7—31/8/34.**G**.
Dar. 19/1—16/2/38.**G**.
Dar. 26/7—28/8/40.**G**.
Dar. 3—28/9/43.**G**.

Dar. 17/9—19/10/46.**G**.
Ghd. 8/11—2/12/49.**G**.
Ghd. 10—29/11/52.**G**.
Ghd. 30/7—24/8/56.**H/I**.
Dar. 18/11/59. *Not repaired.*

BOILERS:
D343.
2534 *(new)* 31/8/34.
4593 *(ex2176)* 28/8/40.
D2015 *(ex2333)* 28/9/43.
8093 *(ex8744)* 19/10/46.
2849 *(ex8721)* 2/12/49.
25709 *(new)* 29/11/52.

SHEDS:
Gateshead.
West Hartlepool 12/12/47.
Borough Gardens 11/4/54.
Gateshead 14/6/59.

RENUMBERED:
8694 2/6/46.
68694 2/12/49.

CONDEMNED: 23/11/59.
Cut up at Darlington.

2178

Darlington.

To traffic 9/1914.

REPAIRS:
Ghd. 31/10/23—15/1/24.**G**.
Dar. 14/2—4/5/27.**G**.
Ghd. 29/11/29—13/1/30.**G**.
Dar. 13/6—11/7/33.**G**.
Dar. 7/10—26/11/37.**G**.
Dar. 23/8—27/9/40.**G**.
Dar. 28/11—23/12/42.**G**.
Dar. 13/5—12/4/45.**G**.
Dar. 18/3—15/3/47.**G**.
Dar. 8/4—2/5/49.**G**.
Ghd. 14/1—1/2/52.**G**.
Ghd. 11/1—10/2/55.**G**.
Dar. 13/10—19/11/59.**G**.

BOILERS:
D345.
HL891 *(new)* 13/1/30.
HL891 reno.HL91 26/11/37.
AW63 *(exJ71 400)* 27/9/40.
2541 *(ex2337)* 23/12/42.
AW54 *(ex2175)* 12/4/45.
D2004 *(exJ71 8294)* 15/3/47.
HL93 *(ex8713)* 2/5/49.
25612 1/2/52.
25636 *(ex68721)* 10/2/55.
25730 *(exJ71 68250)* 19/11/59.

SHEDS:
West Hartlepool.

2178 cont./
Bidston 24/2/39.
West Hartlepool 14/6/39.
York 18/5/40.
Borough Gardens 13/1/57.
Gateshead 14/6/59.

RENUMBERED:
8695 26/5/46.
68695 2/5/49.

CONDEMNED: 2/4/62.
Into Dar. for cut up 3/5/62.

_____

2179

Darlington.

To traffic 9/1914.

REPAIRS:
Ghd. 23/1—1/4/24.**G.**
Dar. 27/5—15/8/27.**G.**
Ghd. 2/5—10/6/30.**G.**
Dar. 15/8—10/10/34.**G.**
Dar. 7/11—5/12/39.**G.**
Dar. 10/4—4/6/45.**G.**
Dar. 2—23/12/48.**G.**
Ghd. 3—29/12/51.**H/I.**
Ghd. 19/4—13/5/55.**G.**
Vacuum ejector fitted.
Dar. 26/6—19/8/59.**G.**
Dar. 12/1/61.*Not repaired.*

BOILERS:
D346.
2549 *(new)* 10/10/34.
D1946 *(ex462)* 5/12/39.
2541 *(ex2178)* 4/6/45.
3527 *(ex8698)* 23/12/48.
3527 reno.25619 29/12/51.
25629 *(exJ71 68300)* 13/5/55.
25717 *(ex68713)* 19/8/59.

SHEDS:
West Hartlepool.
West Auckland 27/5/40.
Stockton 26/6/55.
Thornaby 14/6/59.

RENUMBERED:
8696 26/5/46.
68696 23/12/48.

CONDEMNED: 30/1/61.
Cut up at Darlington.

_____

2180

Darlington.

To traffic 9/1914.

REPAIRS:
Ghd. 25/3—28/5/24.**G.**
Ghd. 18/11/27—20/1/28.**G.**
Ghd. 28/10—1/12/30.**G.**
Ghd. 13/9—3/10/32.**L.**
Dar. 20/8—11/10/34.**G.**
Dar. 7—30/11/39.**G.**
Dar. 25/11—22/12/43.**G.**
Dar. 15/2—20/3/46.**L.**
Dar. 7/5—14/6/47.**G.**
Ghd. 16/5—16/6/50.**G.**
Dar. 17/9—3/10/53.**G.**
Ghd. 3/9—4/10/56.**G.**
Dar. 28/1/60. *Not repaired.*

BOILERS:
D350.
2535 *(new)* 11/10/34.
8089 *(exJ71 494)* 30/11/39.
2847 *(exJ71 239)* 22/12/43.
8106 *(exJ71 8297)* 14/6/47.
3272 *(ex8679)* 16/6/50.
25553 *(exJ71 68297)* 3/10/53.
25740 *(new)* 4/10/56.

SHEDS:
West Hartlepool.
Borough Gardens 31/1/54.
Gateshead 14/6/59.

RENUMBERED:
8697 20/3/46.
68697 16/6/50.

CONDEMNED: 1/2/60.
Cut up at Darlington.

_____

2181

Darlington.

To traffic 9/1914.

REPAIRS:
Dar. 24/1—12/4/23.**G.**
Dar. 18/2—21/5/27.**G.**
Dar. 27/6—26/8/30.**G.**
Dar. 1—25/10/34.**G.**
Dar. 12/12/38—16/1/39.**G.**
GS buffers & hook fitted.
Dar. 3—27/11/41.**G.**
Dar. 9/11—11/12/43.**G.**
Dar. 3—24/5/46.**G.**
Dar. 6—26/11/48.**G.**
Ghd. 17/3—5/4/52.**H/I.**
Dar. 15/11—15/12/54.**C/L.**
Ghd. 18/3—12/4/57.**G.**

BOILERS:
D352.
7959 *(ex571)* 25/10/34.
8098 *(exJ71 451)* 16/1/39.
4588 *(exJ71 272)* 27/11/41.
2543 *(exJ71 980)* 11/12/43.

3527 *(new)* 24/5/46.
8102 *(exJ71 8295)* 26/11/48.
8102 reno. 25634 5/4/52.
25706 *(exJ71 68313)* 12/4/57.

SHEDS:
Darlington.
Sunderland 5/8/39.
York 15/9/57.
West Hartlepool 29/6/58.

RENUMBERED:
8698 24/5/46.
68698 26/11/48.

CONDEMNED: 2/10/61.
Into Dar. for cut up 23/1/62.

_____

2182

Darlington.

To traffic 10/1914.

REPAIRS:
???. ?/?—?/3/22.**?.**
Dar. 18/11/25—23/2/26.**G.**
Dar. 2/6—19/7/28.**G.**
Dar. 28/5—5/8/31.**G.**
Dar. 19/5—18/6/37.**G.**
GS buffers & hook fitted.
Dar. 6/2—18/5/40.**G.**
Dar. 17/10—12/11/42.**G.**
Dar. 15/9—7/10/44.**G.**
Dar. 10/8—7/9/46.**G.**
Dar. 3—19/11/48.**G.**
Ghd. 26/2—15/3/52.**G.**
Ghd. 17—18/3/52.**N/C.**
Ghd. 24/10—1/12/55.**G.**
Dar. 16/12/58. *Not repaired.*

BOILERS:
D353.
7958 *(ex2321)* 18/6/37.
AW75 *(ex2191)* 18/5/40.
3275 *(new)* 12/11/42.
D1334 *(ex2334)* 7/10/44.
HL102 *(exJ71 299)* 7/9/46.
D2013 *(ex8744)* 19/11/48.
25703 *(new)* 15/3/52.
25680 *(exJ71 68284)* 1/12/55.

SHEDS:
Tyne Dock.
York ?/1/27.
Borough Gardens 10/6/56.

RENUMBERED:
8699 26/5/46.
68699 19/11/48.

CONDEMNED: 16/12/58.
Cut up at Darlington.

_____

2183

Darlington.

To traffic 10/1914.

REPAIRS:
Ghd. 1/2—3/4/23.**G.**
Ghd. 18/9—20/11/25.**G.**
Ghd. 19/10—30/11/28.**G.**
Ghd. 1/9—2/10/31.**G.**
Inv. ?/?—13/4/35.**L.**
Inv. ?/?—23/1/37.**H.**
Inv. ?/?—12/7/39.**L.**
Inv. 14/6—23/8/41.**H.**
Inv. ?/?—26/4/43.**L.**
Inv. ?/?—26/8/44.**H.**
Inv. 11/8—1/9/45.**G.**
Inv. 7/5—19/6/48.**G.**
Inv. 13—29/11/50.**L/I.**
Inv. 21/11—11/12/53.**G.**
Inv. 9/7—10/8/56.**L/I.**

BOILERS:
D363.
(C1792) 8099 *(ex Dar.&2328)*
23/1/37.
(C1793) D1144 *(ex2303)* 1/9/45.
2526 *(ex8710)* 19/6/48.
25796 *(ex68749)* 11/12/53.

SHEDS:
Tyne Dock.
Keith 15/3/32.
Kittybrewster 5/4/32.
Keith 14/1/56.

RENUMBERED:
8700 28/4/46.
68700 19/6/48.

CONDEMNED: 2/12/58.
Into Inv. for cut up 2/12/58, but cut up at Kilmarnock 3/59.

_____

2184

Darlington.

To traffic 10/1914.

REPAIRS:
Ghd. 20/3—31/5/23.**G.**
Ghd. 16/4—7/7/25.**G.**
Ghd. 2/11/28—9/1/29.**G.**
Dar. 5/5—16/7/31.**G.**
GS buffers & hook fitted.
Dar. 28/10—29/11/35.**G.**
Dar. 2/5—6/6/39.**G.**
Dar. 11/5—4/6/43.**G.**
Dar. 4—26/6/47.**G.**
Ghd. 3—19/4/51.**G.**
Ghd. 5/3—5/4/57.**G.**
Dar. 5/10/60. *Not repaired.*

2184 cont./
BOILERS:
D362.
2531 (new) 29/11/35.
D2033 (exJ71 179) 4/6/43.
2844 (ex8737) 26/6/47.
25584 (ex8685) 19/4/51.
25662 (ex69008) 5/4/57.

SHEDS:
Sunderland.
Heaton 31/1/27.
Doncaster 14/10/29.
Gorton 22/3/30.
Bidston 27/3/30.
Wrexham 18/10/32.
Bidston 15/11/34.
Wrexham 5/12/35.
Bidston 12/10/36.
Normanton 27/11/54.

RENUMBERED:
8701 26/5/46.
68701 25/6/49.

CONDEMNED: 5/10/60.
Cut up at Darlington.

2185

Darlington.

To traffic 10/1914.

REPAIRS:
Dar. 8/2—30/4/23.**G.**
Ghd. 7/12/27—24/2/28.**G.**
Ghd. 29/10—22/11/31.**G.**
Dar. 19/12/36—23/1/37.**G.**
Dar. 23/12/40—17/1/41.**G.**
Dar. 17/10—8/11/44.**G.**
Dar. 25/11—19/12/47.**G.**
Vacuum ejector fitted.
Dar. 23—31/3/48.**N/C.**
Dar. 19—29/10/48.**N/C.**
G.S. buffers fitted.
Ghd. 2—29/6/50.**G.**
Ghd. 26/1—14/2/53.**G.**
Ghd. 14/3—7/4/55.**G.**
Dar. 7/10—11/11/59.**G.**
Dar. 3/8/61. Not repaired.

BOILERS:
D366.
D1943 (exJ71 285) 23/1/37.
2849 (exJ71 347) 17/1/41.
AW71 (ex2335) 8/11/44.
2545 (exJ71 8282) 19/12/47.
2405 (ex8741) 29/6/50.
25669 14/2/53.
25728 (new) 7/4/55.
25703 (ex68728) 11/11/59.

SHEDS:
East Hartlepool.
West Hartlepool 17/4/39.
Gateshead 12/12/47.
Blaydon 24/12/50.
Heaton 20/5/51.

RENUMBERED:
8702 16/6/46.
68702 31/3/48.

CONDEMNED: 31/8/61.
Cut up at Darlington.

2186

Darlington.

To traffic 10/1914.

REPAIRS:
Ghd. 14/5—20/7/23.**L.**
Ghd. 15/8—4/11/24.**G.**
Ghd. 25/10/27—29/2/28.**G.**
Ghd. 4/11—4/12/31.**G.**
Dar. 28/3—27/4/35.**G.**
Dar. 1/5—9/6/39.**G.**
Dar. 25/10—19/11/43.**G.**
Dar. 9/9—8/10/47.**G.**
Ghd. 30/8—22/9/50.**G.**
Ghd. 4—30/1/54.**H/I.**
Ghd. 16/9—11/10/57.**G.**

BOILERS:
D367.
4586 (new) 4/12/31.
8086 (ex1747) 9/6/39.
D1333 (exJ71 1095) 19/11/43.
3513 (ex8742) 8/10/47.
4075 (new) 22/9/50.
4075 reno.25555 22/9/50.
25743 (new) 11/10/57.

SHEDS:
Sunderland.
Darlington 22/1/34.
West Hartlepool 9/10/34.

RENUMBERED:
8703 16/6/46.
68703 22/9/50.

CONDEMNED: 2/10/61.
Into Dar. for cut up 22/1/62.

2187

Darlington.

To traffic 10/1914.

REPAIRS:
Ghd. 24/4—2/8/23.**G.**

Ghd. 6/10—24/12/26.**G.**
Ghd. 2/9—16/10/29.**G.**
Ghd. 27/7—1/9/32.**G.**
Dar. 30/7—31/8/35.**G.**
Dar. 4/7—8/8/39.**G.**
Dar. 3/2—5/3/42.**G.**
Dar. 25/5—17/6/44.**G.**
Dar. 26/6—19/7/46.**G.**
Dar. 15/9—9/10/48.**G.**
Vacuum brake, heating apparatus & G.S. buffers fitted.
Ghd. 11/2—7/3/52.**H/I.**
Ghd. 27/10—9/11/54.**C/L.**
Ghd. 17/10—18/11/55.**G.**
Dar. 24/9—3/11/59.**G.**

BOILERS:
D369.
4592 (new) 1/9/32.
8112 (exJ71 240) 5/3/42.
D1336 (ex1722) 17/6/44.
2538 (exJ71 1167) 19/7/46.
D1993 (exJ71 8283) 9/10/48.
D1993 reno.25628 7/3/52.
25594 (exJ71 68245) 18/11/55.
25725 (ex68689) 3/11/59.

SHEDS:
Borough Gardens.
Sunderland 31/10/48.
Tyne Dock 29/5/60.

RENUMBERED:
8704 23/6/46.
68704 8/10/48.

CONDEMNED: 16/10/61.
Sold for scrap to G.Cohen,
Cargo Fleet 9/64. Delay in sale
due to a preservation bid which
failed to be completed.

2188

Darlington.

To traffic 11/1914.

REPAIRS:
Ghd. 13/8—16/10/24.**G.**
Ghd. 26/4—16/6/27.**G.**
Ghd. 16/9—28/10/30.**G.**
Dar. 16/2—17/3/34.**G.**
Dar. 4/7—4/8/34.**H.**
New cylinders fitted.
Dar. 14/4—7/5/37.**G.**
G.S. buffers & hook fitted.
Dar. 25/7—22/8/39.**G.**
Dar. 15/12/41—13/1/42.**G.**
Dar. 20/6—8/7/44.**G.**
Dar. 28/8—21/9/46.**G.**
Dar. 30/3—21/4/49.**G.**
Ghd. 8—25/8/51.**H/I.**
Ghd. 27—29/8/51.**N/C.**

Ghd. 30/11—19/12/53.**G.**
Ghd. 23—24/12/53.**N/C.**
Ghd. 30/4—31/5/56.**H/I.**

BOILERS:
D370.
2537 (new) 17/3/34.
D1728 (exJ71 165) 13/1/42.
2837 (ex1736) 8/7/44.
AW56 (exJ71 176) 21/9/46.
2860 (ex8738) 21/4/49.
2860 reno.25609 25/8/51.
25685 19/12/53.

SHEDS:
Borough Gardens.
Gateshead 14/6/59.
Goole 16/8/59.
Hull Dairycoates 8/11/59.

RENUMBERED:
8705 23/6/46.
68705 21/4/49.

CONDEMNED: 10/11/60.
Into Dar. for cut up 11/11/60.

2189

Darlington.

To traffic 11/1914.

REPAIRS:
Ghd. 18/2—14/4/24.**G.**
Ghd. 4/8—30/9/27.**G.**
Ghd. 29/10—10/12/30.**G.**
Dar. 8/5—9/6/33.**G.**
Dar. 16/1—19/2/36.**G.**
G.S. buffers fitted.
Dar. 21/3—9/5/39.**G.**
Dar. 19/8—8/11/41.**G.**
Dar. 16/11—11/12/43.**G.**
Dar. 19/12/45—24/1/46.**G.**
Dar. 7/5—2/6/48.**G.**
Ghd. 21/1—9/2/52.**H/I.**
Dar. 15/5—10/6/55.**G.**

BOILERS:
D372.
E21/6 (ex2318) 9/6/33.
AW71 [exE21/21]
(ex2333) 19/2/36.
8101 (exJ71 495) 9/5/39.
D1993 (ex1733) 8/11/41.
D1943 (ex2336) 11/12/43.
8107 (exJ71 495) 24/1/46.
HL101 (ex8682) 2/6/48.
HL101 reno.25623 9/2/52.
25726 (new) 10/6/55.

SHEDS:
Borough Gardens.
Tyne Dock 29/8/48.

Until 1939, exchange boilers from J71 class led to the use on J72 of water feed being through clack boxes on the barrel. Sunderland, April 1935.

From 1914 the faceplate was the position for injectors feeding water to the boiler.

After Nationalisation, under-footplate live steam injectors were introduced.

Until the 1930's, a wheel and handle was the normal method of fastening the smokebox door. Ferryhill, August 1936.

(above) The four transferred to the Northern Scottish Area in 1932, Nos.2183, 2303, 2310 and 2312, still had the wheel and handle which they kept until BR days. It is possible that No.68719 (ex 2312) kept the wheel to its 24th January 1961 withdrawal because Photo 92 page XX shows it so fitted in May 1959 and it did not have any later works attention.

Nos.542 and 566 had already been changed to two handles before their December 1934 transfer to Northern Scottish Area, as had No.2192 when it went to Southern Scottish Area on 11th February 1939. However, No.2326, which accompanied it, still had a wheel and handle. Kittybrewster, May 1937.

2189 cont./
RENUMBERED:
8706 23/6/46.
68706 2/6/48.

CONDEMNED: 24/10/60.
Into Dar. for cut up 27/10/60.

2190

Darlington.

To traffic 11/1914.

REPAIRS:
Ghd. ?/?—29/12/22.**G.**
Ghd. 18/2—21/4/25.**G.**
Ghd. 30/6—2/9/27.**G.**
Ghd. 26/8—2/10/30.**G.**
Dar. 8/5—13/6/33.**G.**
Dar. 26/11—27/12/35.**G.**
Dar. 1/2—9/3/39.**G.**
Dar. 1—30/9/41.**G.**
Dar. 4—27/4/44.**G.**
Dar. 30/6—16/8/47.**G.**
Ghd. 7—26/5/51.**G.**
Ghd. 12/9—7/10/55.**G.**
Vacuum ejector fitted.
Dar. 26/11/59—14/1/60.**G.**

BOILERS:
D374.
　4589 *(new)* 13/6/33.
　7959 *(ex1749)* 30/9/41.
　HL88 *(exJ71 1153)* 27/4/44.
　2026 *(exJ71 8241)* 16/8/47.
　25587 26/5/51.
　25607 *(exJ71 68256)* 7/10/55.
　25629 *(ex68696)* 14/1/60.

SHEDS:
Borough Gardens.
Eastfield ?/4/25.
Sunderland 6/9/38.
Darlington 23/4/50.
West Auckland 14/9/52.
West Hartlepool 30/4/56.

RENUMBERED:
8707 26/5/46.
68707 26/5/51.

CONDEMNED: 2/4/62.
Into Dar. for cut up 19/6/62.

2191

Darlington.

To traffic 11/1914.

REPAIRS:
Ghd. ?/?—21/12/22.**G.**

Ghd. 14/7—16/9/25.**G.**
Ghd. 7/2—30/3/28.**G.**
Ghd. 8/1—18/2/31.**G.**
Ghd. 28/11/32—24/1/33.**L.**
Dar. 15/10—13/11/34.**G.**
Dar. 3/8—7/9/37.**G.**
Dar. 10—30/4/40.**G.**
Dar. 2—29/10/42.**G.**
Dar. 31/10—25/11/44.**G.**
Dar. 4/11—4/12/46.**G.**
Dar. 21/2—10/3/49.**G.**
Dar. 15/10—2/11/51.**H/I.**
Ghd. 11/1—6/2/54.**G.**
Vac. ejector & steam heat fitted.
Ghd. 29/7—23/8/57.**G.**
Dar. 11/8/61. *Not repaired.*

BOILERS:
D373.
AW73 [exE21/23]
(ex2335) 13/11/34.
AW75 *(ex2313)* 7/9/37.
　8107 *(ex1770)* 30/4/40.
　2844 *(exJ71 482)* 29/10/42.
　2849 *(ex2185)* 25/11/44.
　4587 *(exJ71 8284)* 4/12/46.
　3518 *(ex8745)* 10/3/49.
　3518 reno.25597 2/11/51.
　25698 *(ex68743)* 6/2/54.
　25747 *(new)* 23/8/57.

SHEDS:
Borough Gardens.
Heaton 31/1/54.
West Auckland 11/9/60.

RENUMBERED:
8708 23/6/46.
68708 10/3/49.

CONDEMNED: 11/8/61.
Cut up at Darlington.

2192

Darlington.

To traffic 11/1914.

REPAIRS:
Dar. 27/10—24/12/24.**G.**
Dar. 1/7—23/8/29.**G.**
Dar. 7/11—1/12/33.**G.**
Dar. 29/1—25/2/38.**G.**
Dar. 10/6—14/11/39.**H.**
New cylinders fitted.
Dar. 16—20/11/39.**N/C.**
Inv. 11—25/9/43.**G.**
Cow. 29/4—14/5/48.**G.**
Cow. ?/?—?/6/49.**?.**
Inv. 15/5—22/6/51.**H/I.**
Inv. 26/1—4/3/55.**G.**

BOILERS:
D383.
　2526 *(new)* 1/12/33.
　4591 *(ex542)* 25/9/43.
　4591 reno.25797 22/6/51.
　25792 *(ex68710)* 4/3/55.

SHEDS:
Shildon.
Darlington 7/1/35.
Eastfield 11/2/39.
Kipps 20/1/58.
Polmadie 22/3/61.
Hamilton 24/4/61.

RENUMBERED:
8709 26/5/46.
68709 14/5/48.

CONDEMNED: 26/2/62.
Sold for scrap to G. H.Cambell & Co. Ltd., Glasgow 31/7/62.

2303

Darlington.

To traffic 10/1920.

REPAIRS:
Dar. 30/6—10/9/24.**G.**
Dar. 17/8—3/10/28.**G.**
Dar. 22/9—22/10/30.**G.**
Inv. ?/?—11/4/35.**L.**
Inv. ?/?—1/10/38.**H.**
Inv. ?/?—12/7/41.**L.**
Inv. ?/?—27/12/41.**H.**
Inv. ?/?—7/1/42.**N/C.**
Inv. ?/?—16/12/44.**G.**
Inv. 8/3—10/4/48.**G.**
Inv. ?/?—18/11/49.**H/I.**
Inv. 23/3—13/4/51.**G.**
Inv. 26/3—16/4/54.**G.**
Inv. 26—30/4/54.**N/C.**
Inv. 14—28/12/56.**H/I.**

BOILERS:
D1144.
　1793 1/10/38.
　2526 *(ex2192)* 16/12/44.
　7957 *(ex8749)* 10/4/48.
　D2032 *(ex68717)* 18/11/49.
　25792 *(ex8733)* 13/4/51.
　25798 *(ex8700)* 16/4/54.

SHEDS:
Middlesbrough.
Keith 15/3/32.
Kittybrewster 5/4/32.

RENUMBERED:
8710 28/4/46.
68710 10/4/48.

CONDEMNED: 5/3/59.
Sold for scrap to Motherwell Mcy & Scrap Co. Ltd. 21/8/59.

2304

Darlington.

To traffic 10/1920.

REPAIRS:
Dar. 2/9—30/10/24.**G.**
Dar. 7/9—22/10/28.**G.**
Dar. 24/8—27/9/32.**G.**
Dar. 4/4—13/6/34.**H.**
Dar. 14/6—22/7/38.**G.**
Dar. 13/4—5/5/42.**G.**
Dar. 15/3—14/4/45.**G.**
Dar. 6—28/5/48.**G.**
Vac. ejector & heat app. fitted.
Dar. 21/4—14/5/52.**G.**
Ghd. 23/8—14/9/56.**G.**

BOILERS:
D1151.
　2545 *(new)* 13/6/34.
　2833 *(ex2328)* 5/5/42.
　3882 *(new)* 28/5/48.
　3882 reno.25637 14/5/52.
　25700 *(ex68675)* 14/9/56.

SHEDS:
Middlesbrough.
Darlington 13/6/48.
West Hartlepool 25/7/48.

RENUMBERED:
8711 23/6/46.
68711 28/5/48.

CONDEMNED: 21/8/61.
Into Dar. for cut up 22/8/61.

2305

Darlington.

To traffic 10/1920.

REPAIRS:
Dar. 12/11/25—26/1/26.**G.**
Dar. 26/6—13/8/29.**G.**
Dar. 17/8—14/9/32.**G.**
Dar. 6/4—20/5/38.**G.**
Dar. 26/5—8/8/42.**G.**
Dar. 23/6—19/7/45.**G.**
Dar. 30/7—27/8/48.**G.**
Ghd. 15/10—7/11/51.**G.**
Ghd. 2/5—3/6/55.**L/I.**
Dar. 5/1/59. *Not repaired.*

2305 cont./
BOILERS:
D1155.
D2020 *(exJ71 225)* 20/5/38.
  HL89 *(exJ71 1143)* 19/7/45.
  2535 *(exJ71 8262)* 27/8/48.
  25693 *(new)* 7/11/51.

SHEDS:
Middlesbrough.
Thornaby 1/6/58.

RENUMBERED:
  8712 23/6/46.
  68712 27/8/48.

CONDEMNED: 5/1/59.
Cut up at Darlington.

_____

2306

Darlington.

To traffic 10/1920.

REPAIRS:
Dar. 14/7—23/9/24.**G.**
Dar. 6/7—31/8/28.**G.**
Dar. 20/10—9/12/31.**G.**
Dar. 9/2—16/3/39.**G.**
Dar. 9/9—3/10/42.**G.**
Dar. 11—14/1/44.**N/C.**
Luminous paint on buffer beam.
Dar. 16/10—8/11/45.**G.**
Dar. 3—25/3/49.**G.**
Ghd. 24/9—17/10/51.**G.**
Ghd. 21/3—15/4/55.**H/I.**
Vacuum ejector fitted.
Dar. 21/11/58—9/1/59.**G.**

BOILERS:
D1156.
  2527 *(ex1733)* 16/3/39.
D1161 *(ex2323)* 3/10/42.
  HL93 *(exJ71 501)* 8/11/45.
  2541 *(ex8696)* 25/3/49.
  25717 *(new)* 7/10/51.
  25718 *(ex68676)* 9/1/59.

SHEDS:
Middlesbrough.
Heaton 1/5/55.

RENUMBERED:
  8713 23/6/46.
  68713 25/3/49.

CONDEMNED: 16/10/61.
Into Dar. for cut up 16/3/62.

_____

2307

Darlington.

To traffic 11/1920.

REPAIRS:
Ghd. 6/6—13/8/23.**G.**
Dar. 15/6—17/9/26.**G.**
Dar. 11/4—5/6/30.**G.**
Dar. 24/5—16/6/34.**G.**
Dar. 24/3—28/4/39.**G.**
Dar. 1—24/3/43.**G.**
Dar. 19/3—19/4/47.**G.**
Dar. 19/10—5/11/49.**G.**
Ghd. 18/1—12/2/54.**H/I.**
Dar. 1/8—5/9/57.**C/L.**
Dar. 29/3/60. *Not repaired.*

BOILERS:
D1157.
  7955 *(ex516)* 16/6/34.
AW66 *(exJ71 347)* 28/4/39.
D1155 *(ex2317)* 24/3/43.
AW54 *(ex8695)* 19/4/47.
  2407 *(ex8739)* 5/11/49.
  2407 reno.25691 12/2/54.

SHEDS:
York.
Bidston 8/12/30.
Wrexham 29/6/34.
Bidston 8/10/35.
Wrexham 12/10/36.
Bidston 21/5/37.
Wrexham 9/2/57.
Bidston 1/11/58.
Birkenhead ?/8/52.

RENUMBERED:
  8714 26/5/46.
  68714 25/6/49.

CONDEMNED: 29/3/60.
Cut up at Darlington.

_____

2308

Darlington.

To traffic 11/1920.

REPAIRS:
Dar. 4/8—20/10/23.**G.**
Dar. 27/1—12/4/26.**G.**
Dar. 24/4—19/6/29.**G.**
Dar. 25/10—18/11/32.**G.**
Dar. 23/1—21/2/36.**G.**
Spark arrestor fitted.
Dar. 17/5—26/9/39.**G.**
Dar. 22/6—18/7/42.**G.**
Dar. 20/12/44—20/1/45.**G.**
Dar. 20/6—16/7/47.**G.**
Ghd. 24/1—17/2/50.**G.**

Ghd. 30/6—8/8/52.**G.**
Ghd. 16/4—18/5/56.**G.**
Dar. 26/7/61. *Not repaired.*

BOILERS:
D1159.
  7955 *(ex2307)* 26/9/39.
  2847 *(ex8697)* 16/7/47.
  2399 *(exJ71 68292)* 17/2/50.
  25640 8/8/52.
  25752 18/5/56.

SHEDS:
Hull Dairycoates.
Hull Alexandra Dock 6/4/25.
York 27/5/40.
West Hartlepool 4/3/51.

RENUMBERED:
  8715 2/6/46.
  68715 17/2/50.

CONDEMNED: 26/7/61.
Cut up at Darlington.

_____

2309

Darlington.

To traffic 11/1920.

REPAIRS:
Dar. 18/5—23/7/23.**G.**
Dar. 25/11/25—9/3/26.**G.**
Dar. 25/3—7/5/29.**G.**
Dar. 22/8—19/9/33.**G.**
Dar. 6/9—4/10/37.**G.**
Group Standard buffers fitted.
Dar. 28/1—22/2/41.**G.**
Dar. 19/4—6/6/45.**G.**
Dar. 8/4—18/6/48.**G.**
Ghd. 27/8—15/9/51.**G.**
Ghd. 15/2—4/3/55.**H/I.**
Dar. 6/10—7/11/58.**C/L.**
Dar. 22/2/61. *Not repaired.*

BOILERS:
D1161.
D1336 *(exJ71 1083)* 19/9/33.
  2882 *(new)* 4/10/37.
  8105 *(exJ71 275)* 6/6/45.
  2540 *(exJ71 8248)* 18/6/48.
  25711 *(new)* 15/9/51.

SHEDS:
York.
Darlington 8/8/27.
East Hartlepool 14/11/38.
West Hartlepool 17/4/39.
Heaton 27/5/56.
Darlington 25/1/59.
Hull Dairycoates 3/1/60.

RENUMBERED:
  8716 23/6/46.
  68716 18/6/48.

CONDEMNED: 22/2/61.
Cut up at Darlington.

_____

2310

Darlington.

To traffic 11/1920.

REPAIRS:
Dar. 5/2—4/6/26.**G.**
Dar. 2/8—11/9/29.**G.**
Dar. 14/8—10/9/31.**G.**
Inv. ?/?—?/3/32.**?.**
Inv. 11/12/37—22/1/38.**H.**
Inv. ?/?—8/10/38.**L.**
Inv. 15/2—8/3/41.**G.**
Inv. 9—30/6/45.**H.**
Inv. 29/3—5/4/47.**L.**
Inv. 10—31/12/48.**G.**
Inv. 4—6/4/49.**L/I.**
Inv. 31/3—9/5/55.**G.**
Inv. 25/1—17/2/56.**C/L.**
Inv. 21/10—15/11/57.**L/I.**
Inv. 29/4—12/5/58.**C/L.**
Inv. 3—14/7/58.**N/C.**
Inv. 24—29/9/58.**N/C.**
Inv. 16/3/61.**N/C.**

BOILERS:
D1167.
D1167 reno.C1794 ?/3/32.
D2032 *(ex1734)* 8/3/41.
D1144 *(C1793)* *(ex8700)* 31/12/
48.
  25797 *(ex68709)* 9/5/55.

SHEDS:
Middlesbrough.
Kittybrewster 15/3/32.
Thornton Junction 7/4/34.
Kittybrewster 12/12/43.
Polmadie 3/4/61.
Motherwell 17/5/61.

RENUMBERED:
  8717 28/4/46.
  68717 31/12/48.

CONDEMNED: 8/11/61.
*Sold for scrap to G.H. Campbell
& Co. (Glasgow) 13/6/62.*

_____

No.2192 was the only J72 allocated to Shildon and for shunting at the wagon works it had hinged poles to move vehicles on adjacent roads. It was at Shildon from before the Grouping until 7th January 1935 when it moved to Darlington.

(above) In January 1935 Darlington shed took off the shunting poles but left the brackets in place and these were only removed when this engine was repaired at Inverurie in September 1943. Darlington.

From 1930 when Nos.2184, 2307 and 2320 worked on Birkenhead docks from Bidston shed, they were fitted with a hinged spark arrester at the chimney top. Birkenhead, May 1932.

In February 1936 Nos.462 and 2308, shedded at Hull Alexandra dock, were fitted with spark arresters in the smokebox to work in the pit prop storage yards which were a big fire risk. Alexandra Dock, September 1938.

No.2331 was a York based engine for almost twenty years from new. On 22nd May 1939 it was chosen for fitting with a mechanical stoker, and sent to the Darlington factory of Robert Stephenson & Hawthorns for this to be done.

Ex contractors 21st July 1939, a Nu-Way mechanical stoking system had been fitted. Visual evidence was the two large diameter pipes from the bunker bottom to the firebox, and the pipe up the back of the cab for the exhaust from the steam turbine which worked the apparatus. Regular service was worked to 1947 but the men's representatives would not agree to the single manning it made possible and the apparatus was removed in April 1947.

69

The buffers on the first twenty engines had a parallel shank and hollow spindle.

On the next sixty-five, including the ten built at Doncaster, the buffers were the taper shank type with a solid spindle.

Beginning with No.2184 (8701 later), ex Darlington 16th July 1931, Group Standard buffers and drawhook were fitted when replacement was needed. These increased the overall length of the engine by five inches. Mexborough, June 1947.

2311

Darlington.

To traffic 12/1920.

REPAIRS:
Ghd. 4/10—29/11/23.**G.**
Ghd. 8/9—13/12/27.**G.**
Ghd. 22/4—28/5/31.**G.**
Dar. 12/4—11/5/35.**G.**
Dar. 25/7—29/8/39.**G.**
Dar. 18/5—13/6/42.**G.**
Dar. 21/9—14/10/44.**G.**
Dar. 3—18/5/46.**L.**
Dar. 28/8—27/9/47.**G.**
Ghd. 27/10—22/11/50.**L/I.**
Ghd. 16/12/52—9/1/53.**G.**
Ghd. 26/3—20/4/56.**G.**
Dar. 17/6/58. *Not repaired.*

BOILERS:
D1171.
D2004 *(exJ71 137)* 11/5/35.
  4584 *(ex2174)* 29/8/39.
  2545 *(ex2304)* 13/6/42.
  3275 *(ex2182)* 14/10/44.
  HL88 *(ex8707)* 27/9/47.
  HL88 reno.25570 22/11/50.
  25550 *(ex68735)* 9/1/53.
  25577 *(ex68728)* 20/4/56.

SHEDS:
Sunderland.
Hull Alexandra Dock 31/8/52.
Hull Dairycoates 2/5/54.

RENUMBERED:
8718 18/5/46.
68718 22/11/50.

CONDEMNED: 30/6/58.
Cut up at Darlington.

2312

Darlington.

To traffic 12/1920.

REPAIRS:
Ghd. 11/7—6/9/23.**G.**
Ghd. 28/10/25—5/1/26.**G.**
Ghd. 8/8—28/9/28.**G.**
Ghd. 11/5—12/6/31.**G.**
Inv. ?/?—7/3/33.**L.**
Inv. ?/?—11/6/38.**G.**
Inv. ?/?—23/8/41.**L/I.**
Inv. ?/?—28/3/42.**G.**
Inv. ?/?—19/8/44.**H.**
Inv. 29/12/45—2/2/46.**L.**
Inv. 18/1—8/2/47.**G.**
Inv. ?/?—15/3/47.**L.**
Inv. 24/1—19/2/49.**L/I.**

Inv. 9—25/4/52.**G.**
Inv. 15/1—21/2/53.**H.**
Inv. 1—18/2/55.**L/I.**
Inv. 9—16/11/56.**C/H.**
Inv. 4/7—9/8/57.**H/I.**

BOILERS:
D1177.
C1795 11/6/38.
D1167 (C1794)*(ex2310)* 28/3/42
  8099 (C1792)*(ex2183)* 8/2/47.
  25791 *(ex68750)* 25/4/52.
  25795 21/2/53.
  25800 *(ex69013)* 16/11/56.

SHEDS:
West Hartlepool.
Kittybrewster 15/3/32.

RENUMBERED:
8719 28/4/46.
68719 19/2/49.

CONDEMNED: 24/1/61.
Into Inv. for cut up 31/1/61.

2313

Armstrong Whitworth 391.

To traffic 4/1922.

REPAIRS:
Dar. 21/12/23—29/2/24.**G.**
Dar. 27/5—9/8/27.**G.**
Dar. 13/10—21/11/30.**G.**
Dar. 30/8—30/10/34.**G.**
Dar. 30/6—20/8/37.**G.**
Vacuum ejector fitted. Heating apparatus fitted both ends.
Dar. 24/6—20/8/40.**G.**
Dar. 30/3—29/4/43.**G.**
Dar. 1/5—25/6/45.**G.**
Dar. 19/6—12/7/47.**G.**
Ghd. 31/1—24/2/50.**G.**
Ghd. 8/7—11/8/52.**G.**
Ghd. 12/4—4/5/55.**G.**
Ghd. 6—24/1/58.**H/I.**
Dar. 26/9/61. *Not repaired.*

BOILERS:
E21/1.
AW75 [exE21/25]
(ex2337) 30/10/34.
  2844 *(new)* 20/8/37.
D2010 *(exJ71 492)* 20/8/40.
  2539 *(ex581)* 29/4/43.
  3280 *(ex2323)* 25/6/45.
  2395 *(exJ71 8238)* 12/7/47.
  8112 *(exJ71 8287)* 24/2/50.
  25599 11/8/52.
  25722 *(new)* 4/5/55.

SHEDS:
York.
Gateshead 25/8/37.
Tweedmouth 8/5/60.

RENUMBERED:
8720 2/6/46.
68720 24/2/50.

CONDEMNED: 26/9/61.
Cut up at Darlington.

2314

Armstrong Whitworth 392.

To traffic 4/1922.

REPAIRS:
Dar. 21/9—17/12/26.**G.**
Dar. 31/12/31—2/2/32.**G.**
Dar. 20/5—25/6/38.**G.**
Dar. 23/6—30/7/41.**G.**
Dar. 14/6—7/7/44.**G.**
Dar. 29/1—1/3/47.**G.**
Dar. 20/9—21/10/49.**G.**
Ghd. 24/3—18/4/52.**L/I.**
Ghd. 20/12/54—14/1/55.**G.**
Ghd. 5/2—7/3/58.**G.**
Dar. 21/8/61. *Not repaired.*

BOILERS:
E21/2.
  4583 *(ex2318)* 25/6/38.
  2537 *(exJ71 240)* 7/7/44.
  2849 *(ex8708)* 1/3/47.
  3894 *(new)* 21/10/49.
  3894 reno.25636 18/4/52.
  25692 *(ex68676)* 14/1/55.
  25557 *(exJ71 68267)* 7/3/58.

SHEDS:
Stockton.
Haverton Hill 9/6/30.
Stockton 18/6/30.
Middlesbrough 18/1/37.
Thornaby 1/6/58.

RENUMBERED:
8721 23/6/46.
68721 21/10/49.

CONDEMNED: 21/8/61.
Cut up at Darlington.

2315

Armstrong Whitworth 393.

To traffic 4/1922.

REPAIRS:
Dar. 1/12/26—24/2/27.**G.**

Dar. 10/3—23/4/30.**G.**
Dar. 17/7—16/8/33.**G.**
Dar. 3—30/7/34.**H.**
Dar. 27/2—3/4/36.**G.**
Dar. 12/6—14/10/39.**G.**
Dar. 19/1—21/2/42.**G.**
Dar. 27/6—28/7/44.**G.**
Dar. 8—28/5/46.**G.**
Dar. 19/8—10/9/48.**G.**
Ghd. 14/3—14/4/51.**H/I.**
Ghd. 10/8—2/9/53.**G.**
Vac.ejector & steam heat fitted.
Ghd. 18/6—13/7/56.**G.**
Dar. 25/2/60. *Not repaired.*

BOILERS:
E21/3.
AW72 [exE21/22]
(ex2334) 30/7/34.
D1732 *(ex1718)* 14/10/39.
D1328 *(ex2334)* 21/2/42.
  8094 *(ex2328)* 28/7/44.
  2408 *(exJ71 168)* 28/5/46.
  3888 *(new)* 10/9/48.
  3888 reno.25577 14/4/51.
  25554 *(ex68725)* 2/9/53.
  25695 *(ex69028)* 13/7/56.

SHEDS:
Darlington.
Cambridge 8/8/27.
Peterborough East 14/9/27.
Immingham 26/10/27.
Retford 11/12/27.
Gorton 16/1/28.
Ardsley 2/2/28.
York 16/3/28.
Haverton Hill 29/6/58.
West Hartlepool 14/9/58.

RENUMBERED:
8722 28/5/46.
68722 10/9/48.

CONDEMNED: 29/2/60.
Cut up at Darlington.

2316

Armstrong Whitworth 394.

To traffic 4/1922.

REPAIRS:
Dar. 14/7—23/9/24.**G.**
Ghd. 6/10—24/11/24.**L.**
Ghd. 13/6—9/8/28.**G.**
Ghd. 15/1—18/2/31.**G.**
Dar. 27/10—24/11/33.**G.**
Dar. 14/9—19/10/36.**G.**
Dar. 13/7—12/9/40.**G.**
Dar. 6—29/9/44.**G.**
Dar. 8/7—9/8/45.**L.**
Dar. 2/12/47—2/1/48.**G.**

2316 cont./
Vacuum ejector fitted.
Dar. 14—20/2/48.**N/C.**
Steam heating fitted.
Dar. 27/9—1/10/48.**N/C.**
Group Standard buffers fitted.
Ghd. 9/10—1/11/50.**G.**
Ghd. 22/6—11/7/53.**G.**
Ghd. 29/4—20/5/54.**C/H.**
Ghd. 12/3—6/4/56.**G.**
Dar. 4/4—26/5/60.**G.**
Painted NER. green.

BOILERS:
E21/4.
2544 *(new)* 24/11/33.
7954 *(exJ71 77)* 29/9/44.
3838 *(new)* 2/1/48.
25563 *(exJ71 8314)* 1/11/50.
25551 *(ex68746)* 11/7/53.
25751 6/4/56.
25582 *(ex69009)* 26/5/60.

SHEDS:
Gateshead.
Hull Dairycoates 6/9/37.
West Hartlepool 17/7/39.
Gateshead 12/12/47.

RENUMBERED:
8723 23/6/46.
E8723 20/2/48.
68723 1/10/48.

CONDEMNED: 23/9/63.
Into Dar. for cut up 4/10/63.

2317

Armstrong Whitworth 395.

To traffic 4/1922.

REPAIRS:
Dar. 1/7—18/9/24.**G.**
Dar. 26/10/27—12/1/28.**G.**
Dar. 4/8—1/9/32.**G.**
Dar. 2/4—8/5/35.**G.**
Dar. 29/6—6/8/38.**G.**
Dar. 19/1—26/2/43.**G.**
Dar. 31/10—29/11/45.**G.**
Dar. 24/3—5/5/48.**G.**
Ghd. 24/11—15/12/50.**G.**
Ghd. 3—25/9/53.**G.**
Vac. ejector & steam heat fitted.
Ghd. 3—26/10/56.**G.**

BOILERS:
E21/5.
AW64 [exE21/14]
(ex2326) 8/5/35.
D1155 *(ex2305)* 6/8/38.
2404 *(ex1720)* 26/2/43.
AW60 *(ex2318)* 29/11/45.

3873 *(new)* 5/5/48.
25572 *(exJ71 8282)* 15/12/50.
25675 25/9/53.
25533 *(ex68697)* 26/10/56.

SHEDS:
Hull Dairycoates.
Hull Botanic Gardens 27/4/39.
Hull Alexandra Dock 11/9/39.
York 27/9/53.
West Auckland 13/7/58.

RENUMBERED:
8724 23/6/46.
68724 5/5/48.

CONDEMNED: 19/12/60.
Into Dar. for cut up 22/12/60.

2318

Armstrong Whitworth 396.

To traffic 4/1922.

REPAIRS:
Dar. 22/3—16/7/26.**G.**
Dar. 9/4—23/5/29.**G.**
Dar. 11/5—7/6/32.**G.**
Dar. 30/5—12/7/35.**G.**
Dar. 29/3—27/4/38.**G.**
Dar. 13—30/10/39.**L.**
Dar. 31/10—25/11/40.**G.**
Dar. 10/6—4/8/43.**G.**
Dar. 11/10—8/11/45.**G.**
Dar. 12/1—22/4/48.**G.**
Ghd. 28/8—21/9/50.**G.**
Ghd. 2—24/3/53.**G.**
Ghd. 21/11—16/12/55.**G.**
Dar. 28/3/60. *Not repaired.*

BOILERS:
E21/6.
4583 *(new)* 7/6/32.
8087 *(exJ71 1789)* 27/4/38.
AW60 *(exJ71 1134)* 25/11/40.
8092 *(ex2322)* 8/11/45.
4583 *(exJ71 8311)* 22/4/48.
25554 *(exJ71 8273)* 21/9/50.
25665 24/3/53.
25734 *(new)* 16/12/55.

SHEDS:
Hull Dairycoates.
Hull Alexandra Dock 11/6/39.
Heaton 25/11/39.
Tweedmouth 1/7/56.

RENUMBERED:
8725 16/6/46.
68725 22/4/48.

CONDEMNED: 4/4/60.
Cut up at Darlington.

2319

Armstrong Whitworth 397.

To traffic 4/1922.

REPAIRS:
Dar. 4/1—29/3/27.**G.**
Dar. 28/4—16/6/31.**G.**
Dar. 28/2—30/3/35.**G.**
Dar. 25/8—19/9/38.**G.**
Dar. 27/11/40—2/1/41.**G.**
Dar. 18/8—9/9/44.**G.**
Dar. 10/10—7/11/46.**G.**
Ghd. 28/9—28/10/49.**G.**
Ghd. 26/8—12/9/52.**G.**
Ghd. 25/4—20/5/55.**G.**
Dar. 3/9—12/10/59.**G.**
Vacuum ejector fitted.
Dar. 20/6/61. *Not repaired.*

BOILERS:
E21/7.
AW58 [exE21/18]
(ex2320) 30/3/35.
AW62 *(ex574)* 19/9/38.
D1328 *(ex2315)* 9/9/44.
D1950 *(exJ71 8253)* 7/11/46.
3508 *(exJ71 8300)* 28/10/49.
25638 12/9/52.
25727 *(new)* 20/5/55.
25689 *(ex69003)* 12/10/59.

SHEDS:
Darlington.
Stratford 8/8/27.
Mexborough 10/2/28.
Doncaster 25/2/28.
Mexborough 19/3/28.
York 22/3/28.
Normanton 9/2/58.

RENUMBERED:
8726 2/6/46.
68726 28/10/49.

CONDEMNED: 20/6/61.
Cut up at Darlington.

2320

Armstrong Whitworth 398.

To traffic 4/1922.

REPAIRS:
Ghd. 13/3—14/5/25.**G.**
Ghd. 19/5—16/7/28.**G.**
Ghd. 28/9—2/10/28.**L.**
Dar. 23/2—28/4/31.**G.**
Dar. 17/11—19/12/34.**G.**
Dar. 11/5—4/11/39.**G.**
Dar. 2/2—1/3/44.**G.**
Dar. 17/1—13/2/48.**G.**

Ghd. 7—24/1/52.**G.**
Ghd. 6/8—6/9/57.**G.**
Dar. 25/2/60. *Not repaired.*

BOILERS:
E21/8.
D2022 *(exJ71 492)* 19/12/34.
2397 *(exJ71 8310)* 13/2/48.
25617 24/1/52.
25744 *(new)* 6/9/57.

SHEDS:
Heaton.
Doncaster 30/11/29.
Bidston 3/5/30.
Gorton 25/12/34.
Neasden 1/11/35.
Gorton 23/3/40.
Trafford Park 5/6/40.
Wrexham 8/8/40.
Frodingham 8/3/42.
Gorton 23/6/43.
Bidston 23/6/43.
Wrexham 20/6/54.
Bidston 1/11/58.

RENUMBERED:
8727 26/5/46.
E8727 13/2/48.
68727 25/6/49.

CONDEMNED: 25/2/60.
Cut up at Darlington.

2321

Armstrong Whitworth 399.

To traffic 4/1922.

REPAIRS:
Ghd. 5/6—25/7/24.**G.**
Ghd. 3/6—9/8/27.**G.**
Ghd. 23/1—26/2/30.**G.**
Ghd. 28/9—2/11/32.**G.**
Ghd. 30/12/32—6/1/33.**G.**
Dar. 24/3—17/4/37.**G.**
Dar. 8—29/10/40.**G.**
Dar. 19/4—25/5/43.**G.**
Dar. 11—25/9/44.**G.**
Dar. 29/9—20/10/45.**G.**
Dar. 5/7—6/8/48.**G.**
Vac.ejector & heat app.fitted.
Ghd. 3—26/1/51.**G.**
Ghd. 14/9—9/10/53.**G.**
Ghd. 27/2—22/3/56.**G.**
Dar. 27/4—11/6/59.**G.**

BOILERS:
E21/9.
7958 *(ex566)* 2/11/32.
AW54 [exE21/4]
(ex2331) 17/4/37.
D1999 *(exJ71 260)* 29/10/40.

2321 cont./
  8102 *(ex516)* 25/5/43.
  8097 *(exJ71 1735)* 20/10/45.
  2868 *(exJ71 8240)* 6/8/48.
  25573 26/1/51.
  25577 *(ex68722)* 9/10/53.
  25703 *(ex68699)* 22/3/56.
  25715 *(exJ71 68312)* 11/6/59.

SHEDS:
Tyne Dock.
Borough Gardens 29/8/48.
Gateshead 14/6/59.

RENUMBERED:
  8728 2/6/46.
  68728 6/8/48.

CONDEMNED: 2/10/61.
Into Dar. for cut up 2/10/61.

_____

2322

Armstrong Whitworth 400.

To traffic 4/1922.

REPAIRS:
Ghd. 7/8—9/10/25.**G.**
Ghd. 16/5—22/6/28.**G.**
Ghd. 19/12/30—27/1/31.**G.**
Dar. 22/8—17/9/34.**G.**
Dar. 30/7—2/9/37.**G.**
Dar. 10/6—3/7/40.**G.**
Dar. 25/1—6/3/43.**G.**
Dar. 28/8—25/9/45.**G.**
Dar. 20/1—25/2/48.**G.**
Ghd. 28/12/50—19/1/51.**H/I.**
Ghd. 6/5—5/6/54.**G.**
Dar. 1—29/3/57.**C/L.**
Ghd. 25/9—18/10/57.**G.**

BOILERS:
E21/10.
AW67 [exE21/17]
(ex2329) 17/9/34.
AW61 *(exJ71 1167)* 2/9/37.
  8095 *(exJ71 181)* 3/7/40.
  8092 *(exJ71 1103)* 6/3/43.
  3281 *(ex1732)* 25/9/45.
  8085 *(ex8689)* 25/2/48.
  8085 reno.25576 19/1/51.
  25749 5/6/54.
  25682 *(exJ71 68266)* 18/10/57.

SHEDS:
Tyne Dock.
York 15/9/57.
Ardsley 18/5/58.
Thornaby 25/1/59.

RENUMBERED:
  8729 2/6/46.
  ᴇ**8729** 25/2/48.
  68729 19/1/51.

CONDEMNED: 16/10/61.
Into Dar. for cut up 4/1/62.

_____

2323

Armstrong Whitworth 401.

To traffic 5/1922.

REPAIRS:
Dar. 23/2—5/4/23.**L.**
Dar. 5/10—22/12/25.**G.**
Ghd. 3/6—30/8/29.**G.**
Dar. 4/8—8/9/33.**G.**
Dar. 10/8—11/9/36.**G.**
Dar. 17/10—18/11/39.**G.**
Dar. 17/8—10/11/42.**G.**
Dar. 16/3—14/4/45.**G.**
Dar. 4/2—3/3/48.**G.**
Ghd. 20/11—15/12/50.**L/I.**
Ghd. 21/9—16/10/53.**G.**
Ghd. 18/6—6/7/56.**G.**

BOILERS:
E21/11.
D1333 *(exJ71 1095)* 8/9/33.
D1161 *(ex2334)* 11/9/36.
  3280 *(new)* 10/11/42.
  4594 *(ex2330)* 14/4/45.
D1331 *(exJ71 8303)* 3/3/48.
D1331 reno.25571 15/12/50.
  25570 *(ex68718)* 16/10/53.
  25640 *(ex68715)* 6/7/56.

SHEDS:
Sunderland.
Borough Gardens 31/10/48.
Gateshead 14/6/59.
Tyne Dock 16/8/59.

RENUMBERED:
  8730 26/5/46.
  ᴇ**8730** 3/3/48.
  68730 15/12/50.

CONDEMNED: 7/11/60.
Into Dar. for cut up10/11/60.

_____

2324

Armstrong Whitworth 402.

To traffic 5/1922.

REPAIRS:
Ghd. 31/12/25—5/3/26.**G.**
Ghd. 10/5—24/6/29.**G.**
Ghd. 1—29/5/31.**L.**
Dar. 18/7—5/9/34.**G.**
Dar. 7/11—9/12/38.**G.**
Dar. 26/6—29/7/42.**G.**
Dar. 22/11—19/12/44.**G.**
Dar. 1/7—15/8/47.**G.**
Ghd. 23/5—23/6/50.**G.**
Ghd. 23/11—18/12/53.**H/I.**
Ghd. 22/10—16/11/56.**G.**
Vacuum ejector fitted.
Dar. 26/4/60. *Not repaired.*

BOILERS:
E21/12.
D1157 *(ex2307)* 5/9/34.
D2027 *(exJ71 1198)* 9/12/38.
D2035 *(ex2332)* 29/7/42.
  2544 *(ex2316)* 19/12/44.
D1954 *(exJ71 8300)* 15/8/47.
  2395 *(ex8720)* 23/6/50.
  2395 reno.25690 18/12/53.
  25710 *(ex68732)* 16/11/56.

SHEDS:
East Hartlepool.
West Hartlepool 17/4/39.
Tyne Dock 15/2/41.
Blaydon 14/9/52.
Gateshead 3/2/57.
Tyne Dock 16/8/59.

RENUMBERED:
  8731 2/6/46.
  68731 23/6/50.

CONDEMNED: 9/5/60.
Cut up at Darlington.

_____

2325

Armstrong Whitworth 403.

To traffic 5/1922.

REPAIRS:
Ghd. 8/11—22/12/24.**G.**
Ghd. 15/7—1/9/27.**G.**
Ghd. 5/3—17/4/30.**G.**
Ghd. 29/11/32—23/1/33.**G.**
Dar. 21/8—20/9/35.**G.**
Dar. 23/11/38—3/1/39.**G.**
Dar. 5/8—26/9/41.**G.**
Dar. 23/2—14/3/44.**G.**
Dar. 1—23/3/46.**G.**
Dar. 28/7—3/9/48.**G.**
Ghd. 13/8—1/9/51.**G.**
Ghd. 16—26/11/54.**C/L.**

Ghd. 8/10—9/11/56.**G.**
Vacuum ejector fitted.

BOILERS:
E21/13.
  2524 *(new)* 20/9/35.
  4582 *(exJ71 1831)* 26/9/41.
  8110 *(ex1733)* 14/3/44.
  7961 *(ex2336)* 23/3/46.
  8097 *(ex8728)* 3/9/48.
  25710 *(new)* 1/9/51.
  25583 *(ex69026)* 9/11/56.

SHEDS:
Blaydon.
Heaton 10/4/39.
Gateshead 26/9/48.
Blaydon 22/2/59.
Heaton 25/10/59.

RENUMBERED:
  8732 23/3/46.
  68732 3/9/48.

CONDEMNED: 16/10/61.
Into Dar. for cut up16/3/62.

_____

WORKS CODES:- Cow - Cowlairs. Dar - Darlington. Don - Doncaster. Ghd - Gateshead. Gor - Gorton. Inv - Inverurie. Kit - Kittybrewster. RSH - Robert, Stephenson & Hawthorn. Str - Stratford. Yk - York.
REPAIR CODES:- **C/H** - Casual Heavy. **C/L** - Casual Light. **G** - General. **H**- Heavy. **H/I** - Heavy Intermediate. **L** - Light. **L/I** - Light Intermediate. **N/C** - Non-Classified.

73

In one or two cases only, the drawhook was changed to Group Standard type and wood packing had then to be inserted between the buffer shank and the beam. From 1932 the first twenty were fitted with sandwich type buffer beams, usually only at the front. Nos.68674 and 68683 were exceptional in getting them at the rear. Gateshead, July 1961.

For trial, three were fitted in 1948 with the 'Jay-Gee' smoke eliminator, 68677 (30th April), 68743 (14th May) and 68747 (21st May). External evidence was limited to the extra pipe above the blower connection. All the units were removed in 1951 when these engines were next shopped.

When No.8687 was out of Darlington on 2nd January 1948, it had been fitted with a lamp bracket on the side of the smokebox and red spectacle glass controlled from the cab. It also had extra plates to divert rain from the cab opening but was the only J72 so fitted.

2326

Armstrong Whitworth 404.

To traffic 5/1922.

REPAIRS:
Ghd. 13—27/9/23.**L.**
Ghd. 29/3—2/7/26.**G.**
Dar. 24/9—29/10/29.**G.**
Dar. 9/10—1/11/34.**G.**
Dar. 30/8—29/9/38.**G.**
Cow. ?/?—26/8/44.**H.**
Inv. 23/2—6/4/46.**L.**
Inv. 13/4—3/8/46.**G.**
Inv. 1—28/12/50.**G.**
Cow. 8—9/9/54.**N/C.**
Inv. 16/5—10/6/55.**G.**
Inv. 26/5—22/6/56.**C/L.**
Cow. 24/8—8/9/56.**C/L.**

BOILERS:
E21/14.
 7956 *(ex524)* 1/11/34.
 25793 *(ex68710)* 28/12/50.
 25790 *(ex68717)* 10/6/55.

SHEDS:
East Hartlepool.
Ferryhill 12/7/28.
Darlington 7/11/38.
Middlesbrough 18/11/38.
Eastfield 11/2/39.
Kipps 20/1/58.
Polmadie 27/3/61.
Motherwell 3/4/61.
Hamilton 16/10/61.

RENUMBERED:
 8733 6/4/46.
68733 28/12/50.

CONDEMNED: 16/7/62.
Sold for scrap to P.W.McLellan.
Langloan.10/9/62.

2327

Armstrong Whitworth 405.

To traffic 5/1922.

REPAIRS:
Ghd. 19/5—9/9/26.**G.**
Ghd. 19/7—30/8/29.**G.**
Dar. 6/12/34—19/1/35.**G.**
Dar. 15/4—25/7/40.**G.**
Dar. 4—27/4/44.**G.**
Dar. 26/8—24/9/47.**G.**
Ghd. 30/10—23/11/50.**G.**
Ghd. 2—27/3/54.**H/I.**
Ghd. 12—30/4/54.**N/C.**
Ghd. 17/3—18/4/58.**G.**

BOILERS:
E21/15.
 7954 *(ex512)* 19/1/35.
 2395 *(exJ71 1836)* 25/7/40.
 AW69 *(exJ71 1167)* 27/4/44.
 D1949 *(ex8684)* 24/9/47.
 25567 *(exJ71 8253)* 23/11/50.
 25645 *(ex69007)* 18/4/58.

SHEDS:
East Hartlepool.
West Hartlepool 17/4/39.

RENUMBERED:
 8734 23/6/46.
68734 23/11/50.

CONDEMNED: 2/10/61.
Into Dar. for cut up 23/1/62.

2328

Armstrong Whitworth 406.

To traffic 5/1922.

REPAIRS:
Dar. 1/10—28/11/24.**G.**
Dar. 27/9—29/11/27.**G.**
Dar. 4/11—4/12/30.**G.**
Dar. 4—25/4/34.**G.**
Dar. 15/10—26/11/36.**G.**
Dar. 6/6—10/10/39.**G.**
Dar. 4/3—3/4/42.**G.**
Dar. 17/5—8/6/44.**G.**
Dar. 12/3—14/4/48.**G.**
Dar. 10—24/5/48.**N/C.**
Vac. ejector & steam heat fitted.
Ghd. 9/8—1/9/50.**G.**
Ghd. 3—26/11/52.**G.**
Ghd. 24/5--24/6/55.**G.**
Dar. 30/4—16/5/57.**C/L.**
Dar. 22/10/58. *Not repaired.*

BOILERS:
E21/16.
 8099 *(exJ71 1157)* 25/4/34.
 2833 *(new)* 26/11/36.
 8094 *(exJ71 1140)* 3/4/42.
 7959 *(ex2190)* 8/6/44.
 4594 *(ex8730)* 14/4/48.
 4588 *(ex8693)* 1/9/50.
 4588 reno.25550 1/9/50.
 25707 *(new)* 26/11/52.
 25660 *(ex68742)* 24/6/55.

SHED:
York.

RENUMBERED:
 8735 2/6/46.
68735 14/4/48.

CONDEMNED: 22/10/58.
Cut up at Darlington.

2329

Armstrong Whitworth 407.

To traffic 6/1922.

REPAIRS:
Dar. 25/2—29/6/26.**G.**
Dar. 7/1—13/2/30.**G.**
Dar. 15/8—12/9/34.**G.**
Dar. 25/7—25/8/39.**G.**
Dar. 20/5—1/8/42.**G.**
Dar. 20/12/44—20/1/45.**G.**
Dar. 7/10—7/11/47.**G.**
Ghd. 22/6—3/8/50.**G.**
Vacuum ejector fitted.
Ghd. 9—28/2/53.**L/I.**
Ghd. 2—4/3/53.**N/C.**
Ghd. 28/3—22/4/55.**G.**
Ghd. 10/9—29/10/57.**C/L.**
Dar. 12/4—21/5/60.**G.**
Painted NER green.
Dar. 25—27/5/60.**N/C.**

BOILERS:
E21/17.
 AW53 [exE21/3]
 (ex2315) 12/9/34.
 8104 *(exJ71 1085)* 25/8/39.
 AW68 *(ex2174)* 20/1/45.
 8109 *(ex8740)* 7/11/47.
 8106 *(ex8697)* 3/8/50.
 8106 reno.25676 28/2/53.
 25724 *(new)* 22/4/55.
 25732 *(ex68682)* 21/5/60.

SHEDS:
Darlington.
Borough Gardens 5/11/38.
Starbeck 13/1/57.
York 21/12/58.
Gateshead 16/7/61.

RENUMBERED:
 8736 23/6/46.
68736 3/8/50.

CONDEMNED: 7/10/63.
Into Dar. for cut up 4/11/63.

2330

Armstrong Whitworth 408.

To traffic 6/1922.

REPAIRS:
Dar. 29/6—30/9/26.**G.**
Dar. 1/10—13/11/29.**G.**
Dar. 9/8—27/9/34.**G.**
Dar. 6/9—7/10/37.**G.**
Group Standard buffers fitted.
Dar. 30/5—21/8/40.**G.**
Dar. 9/11—14/12/42.**G.**
Dar. 19/1—9/2/45.**G.**
Dar. 7/5—21/6/47.**G.**
Ghd. 11/4—5/5/50.**G.**
Ghd. 29/9—22/10/52.**H/I.**
Ghd. 17/5—10/6/55.**G.**
Vacuum ejector fitted.
Dar. 2—4/7/57.**C/L.**
Ghd. 21/1—14/2/58.**G.**
Dar. 23/8/61. *Not repaired.*

BOILERS:
E21/18.
 E21/18 reno.AW68 27/9/34.
 AW69 [exE21/19]
 (exJ71 1157) 7/10/37.
 8100 *(exJ71 77)* 21/8/40.
 4594 *(ex1732)* 14/12/42.
 2844 *(ex2191)* 9/2/45.
 2403 *(ex8752)* 21/6/47.
 D2027 *(exJ71 8236)* 5/5/50.
 D2027 reno.25650 22/10/52.
 25593 *(ex68688)* 10/6/55.
 25552 *(exJ71 68273)* 14/2/58.

SHEDS:
Darlington.
Borough Gardens 5/11/38.
Gateshead 14/6/59.
West Hartlepool 11/9/60.

RENUMBERED:
 8737 23/6/46.
68737 5/5/50.

CONDEMNED: 23/8/61.
Cut up at Darlington.

2331

Armstrong Whitworth 409.

To traffic 6/1922.

REPAIRS:
Dar. 4/11/24—8/1/25.**G.**
Dar. 14/6—18/8/27.**G.**
Dar. 24/3—13/5/30.**G.**
Dar. 2—23/2/34.**G.**
Dar. 2/12/36—8/1/37.**G.**
Dar. 7/2—8/3/39.**G.**
RSH. 22/5—21/7/39.
Mechanical stoker fitted.
Dar. 8/7—31/8/40.**L.**
Thermofeed fitted.
Dar. 24—27/11/41.**N/C.**
Dar. 3/12/41—9/2/42.**N/C.**
Fan shaft broken.
Dar. 2/5—3/6/44.**L.**
Dar. 6/2—30/3/45.**G.**
Dar. 1/5—6/6/45.**L.**

Purely shunting engines in Scottish Area were usually fitted with long footstep and a handrail on the bunker but the four J72's sent in 1932 had to await their first works visit for these extras. No.2310 did not get them until 22nd January 1938 when ex Inverurie. Thornton Junction, June 1936.

Until the end of the LNER, sanding was by gravity.

All six sent to the Great North of Scotland section duly got the step and handrail, as did the two sent in 1939 to Eastfield. Kittybrewster, September 1935.

Following experiments at West Auckland shed by a foreman named Downs, in September 1948 at General repairs, three Heaton engines, Nos.68675, 68732 and 68744, were fitted with his design of sanding and immediately transferred to Gateshead shed. A small steam pipe in the box kept the sand dry and fluid to be applied by steam. The rear boxes were also moved from inside the cab to under the running plate.

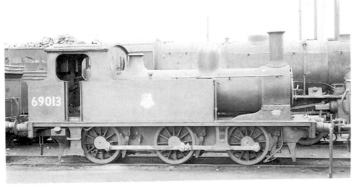

In February 1952, the ER transferred four, Nos.69012, 69013, 69014 and 69015 to ScR. and only 69014 (30th December 1955) has been traced with steps and handrails - see Photo 95 page XX. No.69013 did not have a further works visit after this September 1957 photograph. Note the inner rim of the chimney has been turned off. Other J72's so treated were Nos.2312, 8709, 8733, 68686, 68689 and 68732. There could have been others not recorded. Thornton Jct. September 1957.

Results were sufficiently good for all twenty-eight BR built engines to be fitted with Downs' sanding. Heaton, May 1964.

Until 1937 all eighty-five engines were fitted only with a steam brake and thus worked on goods shunting. York, July 1937.

Apart from Tweedmouth and Carlisle, the class worked on goods shunting based at all the other ex-NER sheds. No.1720 was just one of Hull Dairycoates' docks shunters from 5th November 1932 to 6th September 1937 until during a General repair it was selected for passenger shunting at Newcastle (Central) station, along with No.2313 from York North shed. Dairycoates.

No.2313 ex Darlington 20th August 1937 and No.1720 2nd September 1937, had been fitted with vacuum ejectors, carriage heating apparatus with connections at both ends, and Group Standard buffers with drawhooks. Single red lining was put on their black paint and both were transferred to Gateshead shed. Newcastle Central, May 1939.

Commencing with No.8693, ex works 12th December 1947, by October 1948 vacuum ejectors and carriage heating apparatus had been added to thirteen more J72, Nos.68677, 68678, 68683, 8687, 8689, 8693, 8702, 68704, 68711, E8723 (*see* Photo 74 page XX), 68728, 68735 and 8748. In 1950 three more got these additions: 68679 and 68742 (May) and 68736 (August).

2331 cont./
Dar. 10/12/45—3/1/46.**N/C**.
Dar. 2—25/4/47.**N/C**.
Mechanical stoker removed.
Dar. 28/12/48—3/2/49.**G**.
Ghd. 13/8—1/9/51.**H/I**.
Ghd. 26/10—20/11/53.**G**.
Ghd. 25/2—15/3/57.**H/I**.
Vacuum ejector fitted.

BOILERS:
E21/19.
E21/4 *(ex2316)* 23/2/34.
2860 *(new)* 8/1/37.
AW75 *(ex8676)* 3/2/49.
AW75 reno.25590 1/9/51.
25683 20/11/53.

SHEDS:
York.
*Then used at Darlington works
from July 1939, although not
transferred from York until 24/
11/41.*
Darlington 24/11/41.
Heaton 8/8/48.

RENUMBERED:
8738 20/1/46.
68738 3/2/49.

CONDEMNED: 23/11/60.
Into Dar. for cut up 24/11/60.

2332

Armstrong Whitworth 410.

To traffic 6/1922.

REPAIRS:
Dar. 1/12/24—19/2/25.**G**.
Dar. 25/7—30/9/27.**G**.
Dar. 28/4—7/7/30.**G**.
Dar. 30/1—22/2/34.**G**.
Dar. 15/5—23/6/36.**G**.
Dar. 14/8—9/9/39.**G**.
Dar. 6/6—29/8/42.**G**.
Dar. 31/8—1/9/42.**N/C**.
Dar. 13/9—5/10/44.**G**.
Dar. 27/3—25/4/47.**G**.
Dar. 2—26/8/49.**G**.
Ghd. 22/4—9/5/52.**G**.
Ghd. 9/2—4/3/55.**G**.
Dar. 14/8/59. *Not repaired.*

BOILERS:
E21/20.
8109 *(exJ71 1167)* 22/2/34.
HL94 *(exJ71 1085)* 23/6/36.
D2035 *(exJ71 176)* 9/9/39.
3267 *(new)* 29/8/42.
4589 *(exJ71 165)* 5/10/44.
2407 *(exJ71 8254)* 25/4/47.

3890 *(new)* 26/8/49.
25633 9/5/52.
25653 *(ex69017)* 4/3/55.

SHEDS:
York.
Scarborough 21/12/58.

RENUMBERED:
8739 2/6/46.
68739 26/8/49.

CONDEMNED: 24/8/59.
Cut up at Darlington.

2333

Armstrong Whitworth 411.

To traffic 6/1922.

REPAIRS:
Dar. 4/6—25/8/25.**G**.
Dar. 11/11/27—18/1/28.**G**.
Ghd. 23/11—31/12/31.**G**.
Dar. 6/1—7/2/36.**G**.
Dar. 25/11/39—3/2/40.**G**.
Dar. 7/7—23/8/43.**G**.
Dar. 25—28/1/44.**N/C**.
Luminous paint on buffer beam.
Dar. 5/9—16/10/47.**G**.
Ghd. 2—26/10/50.**G**.
Ghd. 2—27/2/54.**G**.
Ghd. 11/3—5/4/57.**G**.
Dar. 27/7/61. *Not repaired.*

BOILERS:
E21/21.
2030 *(exJ71 278)* 7/2/36.
2015 *(exJ71 252)* 3/2/40.
8109 *(exJ71 1084)* 23/8/43.
2549 *(exJ71 8306)* 16/10/47.
25564 *(ex8703)* 26/10/50.
25609 *(ex68705)* 27/2/54.
25613 *(exJ71 68239)* 5/4/57.

SHEDS:
York.
Darlington 8/8/27.
Middlesbrough 10/6/39.
Thornaby 1/6/58.

RENUMBERED:
8740 20/1/46.
68740 26/10/50.

CONDEMNED: 27/7/61.
Cut up at Darlington.

2334

Armstrong Whitworth 412.

To traffic 8/1922.

REPAIRS:
Dar. 1/12/24—12/2/25.**G**.
Dar. 11/10—16/12/27.**G**.
Dar. 2/10—13/11/30.**G**.
Dar. 7/2—2/3/34.**G**.
Dar. 3/6—31/7/36.**G**.
Dar. 3—27/11/39.**G**.
Dar. 19/1—10/2/42.**G**.
Dar. 31/8—23/9/44.**G**.
Dar. 23/9—23/10/47.**G**.
Ghd. 11/5—9/6/50.**G**.
Ghd. 4—30/12/52.**G**.
Ghd. 6/2—2/3/56.**G**.
Dar. 19/6/59. *Not repaired.*

BOILERS:
E21/22.
D1161 *(ex2309)* 2/3/34.
8109 *(ex2332)* 31/7/36.
D1328 *(exJ71 261)* 27/11/39.
D1334 *(ex512)* 10/2/42.
8111 *(ex2176)* 23/9/44.
2405 *(exJ71 8239)* 23/10/47.
2403 *(ex8737)* 9/6/50.
25704 *(new)* 30/12/52.
25736 *(new)* 2/3/56.

SHEDS:
York.
Hull Alexandra Dock 27/9/53.
Hull Dairycoates 2/5/54.
Hull Alexandra Dock 21/7/57.
Hull Dairycoates 1/2/59.

RENUMBERED:
8741 2/6/46.
68741 9/6/50.

CONDEMNED: 22/6/59.
Cut up at Darlington.

2335

Armstrong Whitworth 413.

To traffic 8/1922.

REPAIRS:
Ghd. 13/3—13/5/25.**G**.
Ghd. 5/1—24/2/28.**G**.
Ghd. 13/2—17/3/31.**G**.
Dar. 31/8—19/10/34.**G**.
Dar. 9/2—15/3/38.**G**.
G.S. buffers & hook fitted.
Dar. 26/2—22/3/41.**G**.
Dar. 24/8—15/9/44.**G**.
Dar. 1/9—2/10/47.**G**.

Ghd. 25/4—19/5/50.**G**.
Vacuum ejector fitted.
Ghd. 21/11—11/12/52.**L/I**.
Ghd. 11/5—3/6/55.**G**.
Dar. 23/12/59—5/2/60.**G**.

BOILERS:
E21/23.
7953 *(ex500)* 19/10/34.
8113 *(exJ71 275)* 15/3/38.
AW71 *(exJ71 1085)* 22/3/41.
3513 *(new)* 15/9/44.
HL100 *(exJ71 8288)* 2/10/47.
4060 *(new)* 19/5/50.
4060 reno.25660 11/12/52.
25620 *(exJ71 68309)* 3/6/55.
25719 *(exJ71 68245)* 5/2/60.

SHEDS:
Blaydon.
Gateshead 29/10/38.
West Hartlepool 12/12/47.
Heaton 18/7/48.

RENUMBERED:
8742 2/6/46.
68742 19/5/50.

CONDEMNED: 16/10/61.
Into Dar. for cut up 26/1/62.

2336

Armstrong Whitworth 414.

To traffic 9/1922.

REPAIRS:
Ghd. 8/1—24/2/25.**G**.
Ghd. 27/7—24/9/28.**G**.
Ghd. 4/11—9/12/31.**G**.
Dar. 13/10—2/11/33.**L**.
Dar. 16/6—8/8/35.**G**.
Dar. 9/1—15/2/39.**G**.
Dar. 5/3—2/4/41.**G**.
Dar. 3—26/11/43.**G**.
Dar. 21/1—16/2/46.**G**.
Dar. 22/4—14/5/48.**G**.
Jay-Gee smoke eliminator fitted.
Ghd. 20/12/50—12/1/51.**G**.
Smoke eliminator taken off.
Ghd. 24/9—16/10/53.**G**.
Dar. 8/9—27/10/55.**C/L**.
Ghd. 4—29/11/57.**G**.
Vacuum ejector fitted.

BOILERS:
E21/24.
D1728 *(exJ71 181)* 8/8/35.
2528 *(exJ71 1863)* 15/2/39.
D1943 *(ex2185)* 2/4/41.
7961 *(exJ71 248)* 26/11/43.
2528 *(exJ71 1198)* 16/2/46.

From September 1953, as vacuum fitted J71 and J77 engines were being withdrawn, their brakes and heating equipment was transferred to J72 class. A process which continued until No.68754 was ex works 12th February 1960. In this period eighteen of the ex LNER steam braked engines were so equipped:- Nos.68686, 68690, 68696, 68707, 68708, 68713, 68722, 68724, 68726, 68731, 68732, 68737, 68738, 68743, 68744, 68746, 68747 and 68754. Darlington, April 1961.

The twenty built by BR during 1949-1950, Nos.69001 to 69020, were fitted with a steam brake only and fifteen of these remained so to withdrawal. Dringhouses, June 1950.

(below) The eight, Nos.69021 to 69028, which BR built in 1951 had steam brakes and vacuum ejectors from new. Darlington, November 1963.

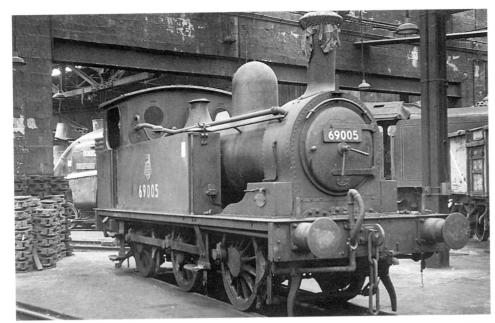

Five of the first twenty BR engines had vacuum ejector and heating apparatus fitted later, Nos.69005, 69008, 69018 in January 1957, 69016 in February 1957 and 69003 in September 1959. Gateshead, July 1961.

Despite more than twenty-five years of moving passenger coaches, this enthusiasts' trip on 29th September 1963 was the only occasion when a screw coupling was used. Even so, No.68736 was only used to haul the empty stock from Heaton carriage sidings to Newcastle (Central) station. Heaton, September 1963.

(below) By Grouping, this was the standard painting for the seventy-five engines, including retention of the large brass number plate.

(above) No.2181, ex works 12th April 1923, was in the chosen LNER black with single red lining, with the number on the tank in 12in. transfers. It is probable that Nos.2183, 2184 and 2185 were the only others to have full points to the new company initials.

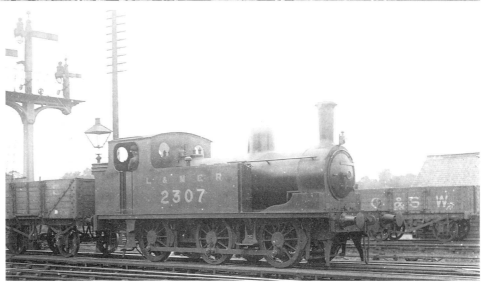

From mid-June 1923 the full points were discarded and, ex Gateshead 13th August 1923, No.2307 was one of the last to have the ampersand included.

Only LNER was being used by the beginning of September 1923 when the suffix D to the number was introduced.

Standard numbering and lettering was used from February 1924 and single red lining was put on until the June 1928 economies took effect. Eastfield. December 1925.

(above) **The ten built by Doncaster in 1925 got standard red lined livery and were the first with brass works plates on the leading sandbox.**

From June 1928 unlined black was standard and remained so except for the passenger station pilots.

2336 cont./
  3875 *(new)* 14/5/48.
  25698 *(new)* 12/1/51.
  25572 *(ex68724)* 16/10/53.
  25555 *(ex68703)* 29/11/57.

SHEDS:
Blaydon.
Heaton 23/3/39.
Darlington 8/8/48.
Hull Alexandra Dock 6/2/49.
Hull Dairycoates 6/12/53.
Hull Alexandra Dock 24/1/54.
Hull Springhead 25/4/54.
Tyne Dock 13/6/54.

RENUMBERED:
  8743 16/6/46.
68743 14/5/48.

CONDEMNED: 2/10/61.
Into Dar. for cut up 6/6/62.

_____

2337

Armstrong Whitworth 415.

To traffic 10/1922.

REPAIRS:
Ghd. 14/4—6/7/25.**G.**
Ghd. 21/4—8/6/28.**G.**
Ghd. 13/2—18/3/31.**G.**
Dar. 10/8—6/10/34.**G.**
Dar. 14/9—12/10/37.**G.**
Dar. 20/3—2/6/40.**G.**
Dar. 20/10—16/11/42.**G.**
Dar. 19/10—11/11/44.**G.**
Dar. 6/7—13/8/46.**G.**
Dar. 1—24/9/48.**G.**
Ghd. 8—27/10/51.**G.**
Ghd. 15—17/11/51.**N/C.**
Ghd. 9—23/7/54.**C/L.**
Ghd. 19/3—13/4/56.**H/I.**
Vacuum ejector fitted.
Dar. 28/9/61.*Not repaired.*

BOILERS:
E21/25.
  2541 *(new)* 6/10/34.
  8093 *(exJ71 168)* 16/11/42.
D2013 *(exJ71 482)* 13/8/46.
  2408 *(ex8722)* 24/9/48.
  25701 *(new)* 27/10/51.

SHEDS:
Blaydon.
Heaton 12/7/34.
Gateshead 8/10/48.
West Hartlepool 5/7/59.
Darlington 2/8/59.

RENUMBERED:
  8744 16/6/46.
68744 24/9/48.

CONDEMNED: 28/9/61.
Cut up at Darlington.

_____

500

Doncaster 1621.

To traffic 2/11/25.

REPAIRS:
Dar. 8—30/11/27.**L.**
Dar. 4/11—15/12/30.**G.**
Dar. 13/8—6/10/34.**G.**
Dar. 14/5—16/6/37.**G.**
Dar. 17/1—12/2/40.**G.**
Dar. 4/3—4/4/42.**G.**
Dar. 28/6—2/8/44.**G.**
Dar. 14—28/4/45.**L.**
Dar. 7/6—6/7/46.**G.**
Dar. 6—26/11/48.**G.**
Ghd. 28/6—18/7/51.**G.**
Ghd. 20/1—12/2/54.**G.**
Ghd. 12/11—13/12/57.**G.**
Dar. 4/9/61. *Not repaired.*

BOILERS:
7953.
  7962 *(ex574)* 6/10/34.
AW68 *(exJ71 1789)* 12/2/40.
D1732 *(ex2315)* 4/4/42.
  2399 *(exJ71 1832)* 2/8/44.
  3518 *(new)* 6/7/46.
D2021 *(ex Sta. Boiler)* 26/11/48.
  25603 18/7/51.
  25688 12/2/54.
  25648 *(exJ71 68287)* 13/12/57.

SHEDS:
York.
Doncaster 1/4/27.
Gorton 12/4/27.
Sheffield 14/5/27.
Annesley 21/5/27.
York *by* 11/27.
Hull Alexandra Dock 31/10/54.
Hull Dairycoates 13/11/60.

RENUMBERED:
  8745 5/5/46.
68745 26/11/48.

CONDEMNED: 4/9/61.
Cut up at Darlington.

_____

512

Doncaster 1624.

To traffic 13/11/25.

REPAIRS:
Dar. 9/8—25/9/29.**G.**
Dar. 5/12/34—12/1/35.**G.**
Dar. 26/7—24/8/39.**G.**
Dar. 17/12/41—23/1/42.**G.**
Dar. 9/2—2/3/44.**G.**
Dar. 14/10—14/11/47.**G.**
Ghd. 10/8—1/9/50.**G.**
Ghd. 31/3—24/4/53.**G.**
Dar. 23/2—20/3/56.**C/L.**
Ghd. 11/2—1/3/57.**G.**
Vacuum ejector fitted.
Dar. 12/12/58. *Not repaired.*

BOILERS:
7954.
D2016 *(exJ71 54)* 12/1/35.
D1334 *(exJ71 403)* 24/8/39.
  8103 *(ex1744)* 23/1/42.
  8089 *(ex2180)* 2/3/44.
  8088 *(exJ71 8314)* 14/11/47.
  25551 *(4076) new* 1/9/50.
  25666 24/4/53.
  25678 *(ex69016)* 1/3/57.

SHEDS:
Neville Hill.
Hull Alexandra Dock 6/2/49.
Hull Springhead 4/7/54.
Hull Alexandra Dock 8/4/56.
Hull Dairycoates 21/7/57.

RENUMBERED:
  8746 12/5/46.
68746 1/9/50.

CONDEMNED: 15/12/58.
Cut up at Darlington.

_____

516

Doncaster 1626.

To traffic 21/11/25.

REPAIRS:
Dar. 7/9—30/10/28.**G.**
Dar. 28/3—24/4/34.**G.**
Dar. 8/9—11/10/38.**G.**
Dar. 6—24/6/41.**L.**
*Damage to smoke box by enemy
action.*
Dar. 18/3—13/4/43.**G.**
Dar. 19/11—14/12/45.**G.**
Dar. 22/4—21/5/48.**G.**
Jay-Gee smoke eliminator fitted.
Ghd. 20/12/50—18/1/51.**G.**
Smoke eliminator removed.

Ghd. 8/9—1/10/53.**G.**
Ghd. 2/7—9/8/57.**G.**
Vacuum ejector fitted.

BOILERS:
7955.
  2543 *(new)* 24/4/34.
  8102 *(exJ71 448)* 11/10/38.
D1323 *(exJ71 1199)* 13/4/43.
D1322 *(ex576)* 14/12/45.
  3877 *(new)* 21/5/48.
  25574 *(ex8740)* 18/1/51.
  25563 *(ex68723)* 1/10/53.
  25609 *(ex68740)* 9/8/57.

SHEDS:
Neville Hill.
Starbeck 1/5/36.
Hull Alexandra Dock 20/5/37.
Bidston 24/2/39.
Hull Alexandra Dock 24/7/39.
Selby 28/5/40.
Hull Alexandra Dock 12/8/40.
Selby 22/8/40.
Hull Alexandra Dock 23/9/40.
Hull Dairycoates 6/12/53.
Hull Alexandra Dock 24/1/54.
Heaton 22/8/54.
Tyne Dock 6/11/60.

RENUMBERED:
  8747 26/5/46.
68747 21/5/48.

CONDEMNED: 23/10/61.
Into Dar. for cut up 6/6/62.

_____

524

Doncaster 1627.

To traffic 30/11/25.

REPAIRS:
Dar. 7/9—29/10/28.**G.**
Dar. 19/8—25/9/31.**G.**
Dar. 14/8—1/10/34.**G.**
Dar. 14/9—12/11/36.**G.**
Dar. 8/7—6/8/40.**G.**
Dar. 27/7—21/11/42.**G.**
Dar. 29/9—21/10/44.**G.**
Dar. 23/12/47—23/1/48.**G.**
Vacuum ejector fitted.
Ghd. 18/6—7/7/51.**H/I.**
Ghd. 26/11—31/12/54.**C/L.**
After collision.
Dar. 23—28/3/55.
Not repaired.
Ghd. 30/3—29/4/55.**G.**
Ghd. 16—20/5/55.**N/C.**
Dar. 22/11/58. *Not repaired.*

BOILERS:
7956.

In August and September 1937, Nos.1720 and 2313, selected for working Newcastle (Central) station, were given full red lining. Newcastle.

When No.1720 returned on 18th May 1940 (as shown) from a General repair, the war had caused two painting alterations. The red lining had gone and the buffers and buffer beam at both ends were white all over to help awareness of them during blackout hours. Low Fell, May 1940.

No.2313 also lost its red lining, presumably when ex works 20th August 1940. From 29th April 1943, it joined those with only NE, effective from July 1942 and ex works 25th June 1945 as shown, it had 6/45 in small figures between the NE and its number. Newcastle, October 1945.

In September 1904, No.1741 was fitted with 18in. instead of 17in. diameter cylinders and these were renewed in January 1937. It worked Dunston coal staiths and was the only one so altered. Note that in 1946 it still had the original taper shank buffers. On Sunday 17th March 1946, Gateshead shed changed its number to 8685.

(below) From January 1946, LNER was restored and ex works 4th March 1948, Inverurie was still applying it, nine weeks after it had ceased to exist officially. Showing the number on the back of the bunker was only done at Scottish area workshops. Kittybrewster, June 1949.

As part of the late LNER decision to apply green lined painting widely, on 24th May 1947 No.8680 (ex 1720) was so painted. Note effect on buffers of only single plate beam at the rear, and that as one of the first twenty it did not have a hand rail across the back of the bunker. This view also shows a footstep injector fitted. Newcastle, October 1947.

524 cont./
AW60 [exE21/10]
(ex2322) 1/10/34.
  8085 *(exJ71 401)* 12/11/36.
  2524 *(exJ71 272)* 21/10/44.
  2542 *(exJ71 8312)* 23/1/48.
  2542 reno.25600 7/7/51.
  25612 *(ex68695)* 29/4/55.

SHEDS:
Hull Dairycoates.
Hull Alexandra Dock 11/9/39.
Hull Dairycoates 22/5/49.
Darlington 28/1/51.

RENUMBERED:
  8748 26/5/46.
E8748 23/1/48.
68748 7/7/51.

CONDEMNED: 1/1/59.
Cut up at Darlington.

_____

542

Doncaster 1630.

To traffic 15/12/25.

REPAIRS:
Ghd. 10/4—27/5/29.**G.**
Ghd. 22/7—25/8/32.**G.**
Inv. ?/?—27/6/35.**L.**
Inv. ?/?—29/10/38.**H.**
Inv. 30/5—27/6/42.**G.**
Inv. 31/3—28/4/45.**H.**
Inv. 9/1—4/3/48.**G.**
Inv. 7/7—18/8/50.**H/I.**
Inv. 9/4—15/5/53.**G.**
Kit. 24/10—2/11/55.**C/L.**
Inv. 12/12/55—13/1/56.**H/I.**
Kit. 9—19/4/57.**C/L.**
Inv. 21—31/10/58.**C/L.**

BOILERS:
  7957.
  4591 *(new)* 25/8/32.
  7957 *(ex566)* 27/6/42.
  4582 *(exDar & J71 8252)* 4/3/
48.
25670 15/5/53.

SHEDS:
Sunderland.
Kittybrewster 22/12/34.

RENUMBERED:
  8749 31/3/46.
68749 18/8/50.

CONDEMNED: 16/8/60.
Into Inv. for cut up 19/8/60.

_____

566

Doncaster 1631.

To traffic 16/12/25.

REPAIRS:
Ghd. 6/5—21/6/29.**G.**
Ghd. 16/9—17/10/32.**G.**
Inv. ?/?—24/1/36.**L.**
Inv. 2/7—6/8/38.**H.**
Inv. 11/4—2/5/42.**G.**
Inv. 30/12/44—20/1/45.**H.**
Inv. 27/9—18/10/47.**G.**
Inv. ?/?—14/5/49.**L/I.**
Inv. 5—22/11/51.**G.**
Inv. 22/6—13/7/54.**H/I.**
Inv. 30/5—29/6/56.**C/L.**
Inv. 2—23/8/57.**G.**

BOILERS:
  7958.
  7957 *(ex542)* 17/10/32.
(C1795) D1177 *(ex2312)* 2/5/42.
(C1794) D1167 *(ex8719)* 18/10/
47.
25794 *(ex68710)* 22/11/51.
25637 *(ex68711)* 23/8/57.

SHEDS:
Sunderland.
Kittybrewster 22/12/34.
Polmadie 3/4/61.
Motherwell 17/5/61.
Hamilton 16/10/61.
Dumfries 25/6/62.

RENUMBERED:
  8750 12/4/46.
68750 14/5/49.

CONDEMNED: 17/12/62.
Sold for scrap to J.McWilliam,
Shettleston, 12/62.

_____

571

Doncaster 1633.

To traffic 22/12/25.

REPAIRS:
Dar. 19/3—30/4/29.**G.**
Dar. 2/9—15/10/34.**G.**
Dar. 28/12/39—9/2/40.**G.**
Dar. 29/3—19/4/44.**G.**
Dar. 26/6—9/8/47.**G.**
Ghd. 7/3—6/4/50.**G.**
Ghd. 8—31/12/52.**G.**
Ghd. 28/11—21/12/55.**G.**
Dar. 15/5/59. *Not repaired.*

BOILERS:
  7959.

2542 *(new)* 15/10/34.
  8103 *(ex512)* 19/4/44.
D2033 *(ex8701)* 9/8/47.
  2539 *(exJ71 8280)* 6/4/50.
25661 31/12/52.
25735 *(new)* 21/12/55.

SHEDS:
Hull Dairycoates.
Hull Alexandra Dock 11/6/39.
Hull Dairycoates 7/3/54.

RENUMBERED:
  8751 23/6/46.
68751 6/4/50.

CONDEMNED: 18/5/59.
Cut up at Darlington.

_____

574

Doncaster 1634.

To traffic 22/12/25.

REPAIRS:
Dar. 30/9—31/10/30.**G.**
Dar. 1/8—7/9/34.**G.**
Dar. 11/5—15/6/38.**G.**
Dar. 21/3—18/4/41.**G.**
Dar. 6/12/44—6/1/45.**G.**
Dar. 19/4—17/5/47.**G.**
Dar. 5/12/49—2/1/50.**G.**
Dar. 9—11/1/50.**N/C.**
Ghd. 9/9—2/10/52.**G.**
Ghd. 14/7—5/8/55.**G.**
Ghd. 29/10—14/11/57.**C/H.**
Dar. 1/2/60. *Not repaired.*

BOILERS:
  7962.
AW62 [exE21/12]
(ex2324) 7/9/34.
  HL97 *(exJ71 240)* 15/6/38.
D2026 *(exJ71 1861)* 18/4/41.
  2403 *(exJ71 533)* 6/1/45.
  3267 *(exJ71 8257)* 17/5/47.
  2536 *(ex8680)* 2/1/50.
25632 *(exJ71 8231)* 2/10/52.
25568 *(ex68685)* 5/8/55.
25698 *(ex68708)* 14/11/57.

SHEDS:
Neville Hill.
Hull Dairycoates 11/2/26.
Hull Alexandra Dock 20/6/39.
Hull Dairycoates 21/7/57.

RENUMBERED:
  8752 23/6/46.
68752 2/1/50.

CONDEMNED: 1/2/60.
Cut up at Darlington.

576

Doncaster 1635.

To traffic 24/12/25.

REPAIRS:
Dar. 3/4—28/5/29.**G.**
Dar. 1/8—12/9/34.**G.**
Dar. 10/8—5/9/39.**G.**
Dar. 6/2—6/3/43.**G.**
Dar. 31/10—29/11/45.**G.**
Dar. 10/4—6/5/48.**G.**
Ghd. 6—30/11/50.**G.**
Ghd. 23/4—16/5/53.**G.**
Ghd. 26/3—26/4/57.**H/I.**
Dar. 20/3—7/4/59.**C/L.**
Dar. 8/8/60. *Not repaired.*

BOILERS:
  7960.
D2016 *(ex512)* 5/9/39.
D1322 *(exJ71 237)* 6/3/43.
D1161 *(ex2306)* 29/11/45.
  7959 *(ex8735)* 6/5/48.
  3838 *(ex68723)* 30/11/50.
  25663 16/5/53.

SHEDS:
Hull Alexandra Dock.
Selby 4/6/40.
Hull Alexandra Dock 22/8/40.
Hull Dairycoates 16/5/54.

RENUMBERED:
  8753 23/6/46.
68753 6/5/48.

CONDEMNED: 15/8/60.
Cut up at Darlington.

_____

581

Doncaster 1636.

To traffic 28/12/25.

REPAIRS:
Dar. 16/8—7/10/29.**G.**
Dar. 7/6—11/7/33.**G.**
Dar. 16/6—11/7/36.**G.**
Dar. 15/12/39—10/1/40.**G.**
Dar. 3—30/3/43.**G.**
Dar. 27/4—17/5/46.**G.**
Ghd. 22/8—16/9/49.**G.**
Ghd. 11/7—11/8/51.**C/L.**
Ghd. 3—24/12/52.**G.**
Ghd. 29/5—28/6/56.**H/I.**
Dar. 5/1—16/2/60.**G.**
Vacuum ejector fitted.

BOILERS:
  7961.
  2539 *(exJ71 301)* 10/1/40.

581 cont./
8095 *(ex2322)* 30/3/43.
2534 *(exJ71 8285)* 17/5/46.
8094 *(exJ71 8268)* 16/9/49.
25708 *(new)* 24/12/52.
25709 *(ex68694)* 16/2/60.

SHEDS:
Darlington.
Ferryhill 2/2/26.
Darlington 7/11/38.
Middlesbrough 18/11/38.
Darlington 29/7/56.
Thornaby 3/9/61.
Darlington 25/2/62.

RENUMBERED:
8754 23/6/46.
68754 16/9/49.

CONDEMNED: 2/4/62.
Into Dar. for cut up 18/4/62.

69001

Darlington 2082.

To traffic 31/10/49.

REPAIRS:
Dar. 2—5/11/49.**N/C.**
For official photograph.
Ghd. 17/6—8/7/52.**G.**
Dar. 15/4—7/5/55.**G.**
Ghd. 3/12/58—23/1/59.**G.**
Dar. 26/3—18/4/63.**C/L.**

BOILERS:
3897.
25624 8/7/52.
25714 *(exJ71 68230)* 7/5/55.
25748 *(ex68673)* 23/1/59.

SHEDS:
Hull Alexandra Dock.
Heaton 26/6/55.
Blaydon 16/6/57.
Gateshead 22/2/59.

CONDEMNED: 23/9/63.
Into Dar. for cut up 15/10/63.

69002

Darlington 2083.

To traffic 2/11/49.

REPAIRS:
Ghd. 12—29/8/52.**G.**
Ghd. 25/2—20/3/54.**C/L.**
Ghd. 3—21/3/58.**G.**
Dar. 22/1—11/3/60.**N/C.**

BOILERS:
3900.
25639 29/8/52.
25686 *(exJ71 68253)* 21/3/58.

SHEDS:
Hull Alexandra Dock.
Sunderland 31/8/52.
West Auckland 11/9/60.
Darlington 1/1/61.
Thornaby 1/10/61.
Darlington 25/2/62.

CONDEMNED: 1/10/62.
Into Dar. for cut up 17/10/62.

69003

Darlington 2084.

To traffic 8/11/49.

REPAIRS:
Ghd. 26/8—13/9/52.**G.**
Ghd. 20/7—12/8/55.**G.**
Ghd. 25/11—17/12/57.**C/H.**
Dar. 31/7—2/9/59.**G.**
Vac. ejector & steam heat fitted.

BOILERS:
4010.
25642 13/9/52.
25676 *(ex68736)* 12/8/55.
25689 *(ex69018)* 17/12/57.
25657 *(ex69022)* 2/9/59.

SHEDS:
Hull Alexandra Dock.
York 21/2/60.
West Hartlepool 29/10/61.

CONDEMNED: 28/12/63.
Sold for scrap to G.Cohen & Sons, Cargo Fleet, 8/64.

69004

Darlington 2085.

To traffic 17/11/49.

REPAIRS:
Ghd. 17/8—4/9/53.**L/I.**
Ghd. 19/12/56—18/1/57.**C/H.**
Ghd. 11—29/8/58.**G.**

BOILERS:
4012.
4012 reno.25684 4/9/53.
25699 29/8/58.

SHEDS:
Darlington.

Thornaby 13/8/61.
Darlington 25/2/62.
Gateshead 25/3/62.

CONDEMNED: 23/9/63.
Into Dar. for cut up 15/10/63.

69005

Darlington 2086.

To traffic 17/11/49.

REPAIRS:
Ghd. 3—15/11/51.**C/L.**
Ghd. 3—21/11/52.**L/I.**
Ghd. 6—23/6/55.**C/H.**
Ghd. 10/12/56—4/1/57.**G.**
Vacuum ejector fitted.
Dar. 28/12/61—31/1/62.**G.**

BOILERS:
4014.
4014 reno.25658 21/11/52.
25673 *(ex68679)* 4/1/57.
25607 *(ex68707)* 31/1/62.

SHEDS:
Gateshead.
North Blyth 26/10/64.

RENUMBERED:
DEPT'L 58 26/10/64.

CONDEMNED: 7/10/67.
Sold for scrap to W. Willoughby, Choppington, 10/1/68.

69006

Darlington 2087.

To traffic 24/11/49.

REPAIRS:
Ghd. 8/12/52—7/1/53.**H/I.**
Ghd. 2—27/1/56.**G.**
Dar. 12/4/56.**N/C.**
Dar. 23/2—16/3/59.**C/H.**
Dar. 1/11—3/12/60.**G.**
Dar. 2—16/10/61.**C/L.**

BOILERS:
4016.
4016 reno.25664 7/1/53.
25679 *(ex68693)* 27/1/56.
25667 *(exJ71 68232)* 16/3/59.
25740 *(ex68697)* 3/12/60.

SHEDS:
Middlesbrough.
Thornaby 1/6/58.
Darlington 25/2/62.

CONDEMNED: 9/12/63.
Into Dar. for cut up 31/12/63.

69007

Darlington 2088.

To traffic 24/11/49.

REPAIRS:
Ghd. 13—29/8/52.**L/I.**
Ghd. 9/1—1/2/57.**C/L.**
Ghd. 3—28/2/58.**G.**

BOILERS:
4018.
4018 reno.25645 29/8/52.
25619 *(ex68696)* 28/2/58.

SHEDS:
West Auckland.
Sunderland 31/8/52.
West Auckland 8/3/59.
Darlington 1/1/61.
Thornaby 1/10/61.

CONDEMNED: 1/10/62.
Into Dar. for cut up 19/10/62.

69008

Darlington 2089.

To traffic 9/12/49.

REPAIRS:
Ghd. 1—19/12/52.**L/I.**
Ghd. 4—25/1/57.**G.**
Vacuum ejector fitted.
Dar. 26/10—1/12/61.**G.**

BOILERS:
4020.
4020 reno.25662 19/12/52.
25564 *(exJ71 68240)* 25/1/57.
25705 *(ex69020)* 1/12/61.

SHEDS:
Tyne Dock.
Goole 16/6/57.
Hull Dairycoates 21/12/58.
York 21/2/60.
Heaton 1/10/61.
Gateshead 16/6/63.

CONDEMNED: 9/12/63.
Sold for scrap to T. J.Thompson, Stockton-on-Tees, 12/64.

Ex Darlington works 29th October 1949, it was still in LNER lined green but with the BR emblem in place of LNER and with standard cream painted 10in. numbers and fitted with a smokebox number plate. Newcastle, June 1950.

From its next shopping, ex Gateshead works 14th March 1952, it was in black but with red, cream and grey BR lining although limited to just a rectangular panel on the tank and bunker. Newcastle, July 1952.

Similarly painted when ex Gateshead works 16th August 1957, it now had the BR crest in place of the emblem although of the version which offended in heraldry by the lion facing the wrong way.

Although it continued as Newcastle station pilot to withdrawal on 16th October 1961, from its final repair on 15th December 1959, it was given no special treatment by Darlington, being simply in unlined black.

Nine of the class acquired the BR E prefix to their number in 1948, three of them still as LNER: Nos.E8687 (4th March), E8693 (17th March) and E8723 (20th February) at Non/ Classified repairs as they had been called in just to have carriage heating equipment fitted. Six more got the E and BRITISH RAILWAYS following a General repair: E8672 (11th March), E8682 (4th March), E8727 (13th February), E8729 (25th February), E8730 (3rd March), E8748 (23rd January).

After the number 6 replaced the E prefix, No.68692 being the first J72 on 25th March 1948, twelve of the class got this style with the number still painted on the buffer beam. York.

(below) No.68716, ex works 18th June 1948, was the first J72 to be fitted with a smokebox number plate. Note that the early castings had the modified figure 6. Darlington.

Only three weeks later, when No.68683 was ex works 9th July 1948, the figures had been changed from 12in. to 10in. which then became standard but the modified 6 (and 9) were still being used. West Hartlepool, August 1950.

By the end of October 1948, Darlington smokebox plates had the correct Gill sans 6 and 9. No.68702 got its plate on 29th October 1948 when called into Darlington for G.S. buffers to be fitted. After the BRITISH RAILWAYS lettering was superseded by the emblem in September 1949, this was the standard style until 1957. Heaton, May 1956.

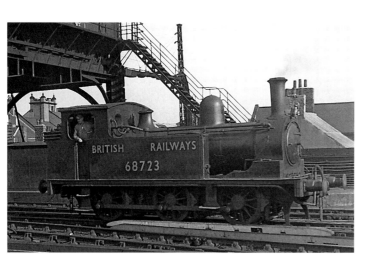

When No.68723 was out of Darlington on 1st October 1948, with Group Standard buffers fitted, it had been repainted and renumbered from E8723 to 68723 and the correct Gill sans 6 was used, but note that no smokebox plate was put on. Newcastle, July 1949.

Because the first of the BR built engines was not ex works until 31st October 1949, the change to the emblem had already been made. Alexandra Dock, Hull, December 1949.

A smokebox number plate was usually only fitted at Darlington so when 68735 was ex Gateshead 1st September 1950, after a General repair, it did not have a plate although the door had been drilled for one to be fitted. York.

All J72 class had the smaller (15$\frac{1}{2}$in.) size emblem and they were handed to face forward on both sides of the engine. Sunderland, August 1960.

Engines shedded at Heaton had some duties which took them under the overhead wiring of the Newcastle Quayside line. Electrification warning signs were put on the front end of their side tanks. Heaton, July 1961.

From mid-1957 the emblem was superseded by the BR crest, No.68750 getting it ex Inverurie 23rd August 1957. For more than a year a wrong handed version was applied which had the lion facing to the right on this side of the engine resulting in a serious heraldic faux pas. Dumfries, May 1963.

(below) During 1959 change was made to conform to correct heraldic principles, the same crest then being used on both sides. At least fifty-three never carried the 1957 crest. Darlington, April 1961.

From late 1960, Darlington reverted to 12in. figures for the tank side number and they never adopted the bunker position after the NER brass plate was removed. Gateshead, July 1963.

Whilst still LNER, the eight maintained by Cowlairs and Inverurie got similar lining to those dealt with by Darlington. Between 28th September 1943 and 1st September 1945 they were all reduced to just NE but in 12in. shaded transfers. Eastfield, June 1947.

(below) Only three had the LNER restored: 8733 (3rd August 1946), 8719 (8th February 1947) and 8750 (18th October 1947), before Nationalisation, but somewhat surprisingly - *see* page 93, middle - No.8749, ex Inverurie 4th March 1948, had this full LNER style. Note both 8709 and 8719 have had the inner rim of the chimney turned off. Kittybrewster.

69009

Darlington 2090.

To traffic 16/12/49.

REPAIRS:
Ghd. 20/5—6/6/52.**G.**
Ghd. 27/5—26/6/54.**C/L.**
Ghd. 25/10—19/11/55.**H/I.**
Ghd. 28/3—3/5/57.**C/H.**
Dar. 19/11—22/12/59.**G.**

BOILERS:
 4021.
25631 6/6/52.
25582 *(ex69023)* 3/5/57.
25728 *(ex68702)* 22/12/59.

SHEDS:
Hull Alexandra Dock.
Hull Dairycoates 13/11/60.
West Hartlepool 20/1/63.

CONDEMNED: 16/9/63.
Into Dar. for cut up 1/10/63.

69010

Darlington 2091.

To traffic 20/12/49.

REPAIRS:
Ghd. 5—24/1/53.**H/I.**
Ghd. 7/11—2/12/55.**G.**
Dar. 27/5—22/6/59.**G.**

BOILERS:
 4023.
 4023 reno.25672 24/1/53.
25615 *(ex68683)* 2/12/55.
25680 *(ex68699)* 22/6/59.

SHEDS:
Hull Dairycoates.
Hull Alexandra Dock 8/3/53.
Hull Dairycoates 13/11/60.

CONDEMNED: 1/10/62.
Into Dar. for cut up 4/4/63.

69011

Darlington 2092.

To traffic 22/12/49.

REPAIRS:
Ghd. 17/2—13/3/53.**H/I.**
Ghd. 24/11—21/12/55.**G.**
Ghd. 30/8—18/9/57.**C/H.**
Dar. 18/3—23/4/60.**H/I.**

BOILERS:
 4024.
 4024 reno.25677 13/3/53.
25654 *(exJ71 68280)* 21/12/55.
25745 *(new)* 18/9/57.

SHEDS:
Hull Dairycoates.
Hull Alexandra Dock 8/3/53.
Hull Dairycoates 13/11/60.
West Hartlepool 20/1/63.

CONDEMNED: 9/12/63.
Sold for scrap to G.Cohen & Sons, Cargo Fleet, 9/64.

69012

Darlington 2093.

To traffic 23/12/49.

REPAIRS:
Dar. 7/1/50.**N/C.**
Inv. 7/12/53—15/1/54.**G.**
Inv. 4—5/2/54.**N/C.**
Inv. 3—31/3/58.**L/I.**

BOILERS:
4026.
4026 reno.25799 15/1/54.

SHEDS:
Doncaster.
Ipswich 28/5/50.
Thornton Junction 3/2/52.

CONDEMNED: 21/2/61.
Into Inv. for cut up 3/3/61.

69013

Darlington 2094.

To traffic 28/12/49.

REPAIRS:
Inv. 14—31/10/52.**L/I.**
Inv. 6—31/10/53.**L/I.**
Inv. 2—25/5/56.**G.**

BOILERS:
 4029.
 4029 reno.25800 31/10/52.
25802 *(ex69014)* 25/5/56.

SHEDS:
Doncaster.
Ipswich 28/5/50.
Thornton Junction 3/2/52.
St Margaret's 17/12/57.
Polmadie 1/3/61.
Motherwell 16/6/61.

CONDEMNED: 22/1/62.
Sold for scrap to G.H.Cambell & Co. (Glasgow) Ltd.20/6/62.

69014

Darlington 2095.

To traffic 29/12/49.

REPAIRS:
Inv. 30/11—30/12/55.**G.**
In to store 30/3/59.

BOILERS:
 4032.
25793 *(ex68733)* 30/12/55.

SHEDS:
Doncaster.
St Margaret's 3/2/52.

CONDEMNED: 19/2/62.
In for c/u 24/2/62, but sold for scrap to W.H.Arnot, Young & Co. Carmyle, 29/8/63.

69015

Darlington 2096.

To traffic 30/12/49.

REPAIRS:
Inv. 1/7—26/8/54.**G.**
Inv. 3/6—12/7/57.**L/I.**
Cow. 12—31/8/57.**C/L.**

BOILERS:
4031.
4031 reno.25801 26/8/54.

SHEDS:
Doncaster.
Sheffield 30/8/50.
Doncaster 19/9/50.
Parkhead 3/2/52.
Motherwell 23/2/61.

CONDEMNED: 14/9/61.
C/u at Heatheryknowe 18/11/61.

69016

Darlington 2097.

To traffic 9/1/50.

REPAIRS:
Ghd. 17/3—9/4/53.**L/I.**
Ghd. 8/1—1/2/57.**G.**
Vacuum ejector fitted.

Dar. 27/12/61—27/1/62.**G.**

BOILERS:
 4034.
 4034 reno.25678 9/4/53.
25742 *(new)* 1/2/57.
25726 *(ex68706)* 27/1/62.

SHEDS:
York.
Scarborough 22/1/50.
York 21/12/58.
Thornaby 29/10/61.
West Hartlepool 29/9/63.
Gateshead 29/12/63.

CONDEMNED: 26/10/64.
Sold for scrap T.J. Thompson, Stockton-on-Tees, 12/64.

69017

Darlington 2098.

To traffic 13/1/50.

REPAIRS:
Ghd. 6—23/10/52.**L/I.**
Ghd. 18/1—11/2/55.**G.**
Ghd. 7/10—1/11/57.**H/I.**

BOILERS:
 4037.
 4037 reno.25653 23/10/52.
25606 *(ex68686)* 11/2/55.

SHEDS:
Darlington.
Borough Gardens 11/6/50.
Gateshead 14/6/59.
West Hartlepool 5/7/59.
Darlington 19/7/59.
Thornaby 1/10/61.

CONDEMNED: 30/4/62.
Into Dar. for cut up 19/6/62.

69018

Darlington 2099.

To traffic 19/1/50.

REPAIRS:
Ghd. 26/10—13/11/53.**L/I.**
Ghd. 29/12/56—18/1/57.**G.**
Vacuum ejector fitted.

BOILERS:
 4039.
 4039 reno.25689 13/11/53.
25681 *(ex68690)* 18/1/57.

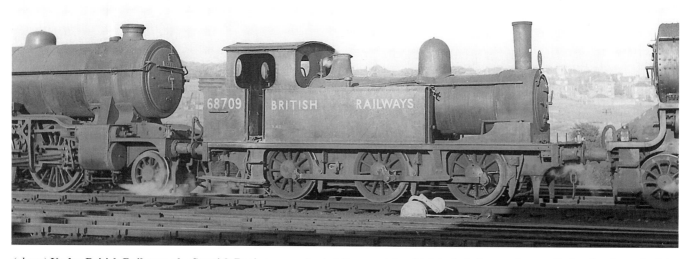

(above) Under British Railways, the Scottish Region soon adopted its own style which included a number on the bunker instead of the tank. Although 68709 (as 2192) had been at Eastfield shed from 11th February 1939, only when ex Cowlairs on 14th May 1948 was it fitted with the shunter's step and handrail. The latter was shorter and higher than normal, causing the number and lettering to look awkwardly placed.

On 10th April 1948 Inverurie sent out No.68710 and they had put the number on the bunker so now dispensed with a number on the back of the bunker.

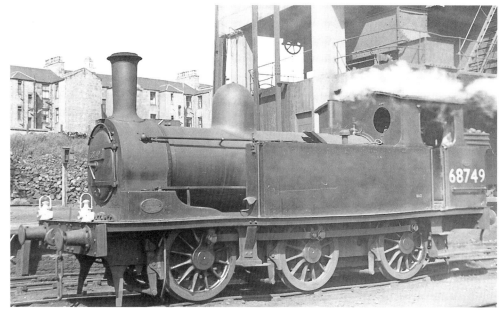

Nos.68733 and 68749 never had the BRITISH RAILWAYS put on. No.68749 had plain tanks when ex works 18th August 1950 and No.68733 had the emblem when out on 28th December 1950. Kittybrewster.

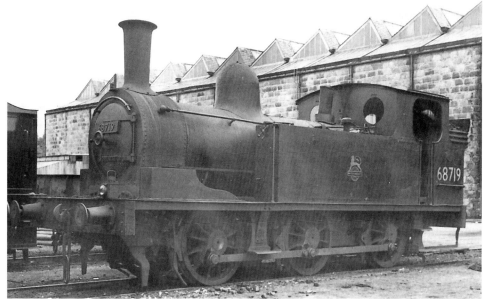

All eight duly got the emblem but the spread was from No.68733 on 28th December 1950 to No.68717 on 9th May 1955. None acquired the 1957 BR crest. Note No.68719 still has a wheel on the smokebox door in this 16th May 1959 illustration; it was withdrawn on 24th January 1961 without further works attention. Inverurie works. Inverurie, May 1959.

On 3rd February 1952, four of the 1949 BR batch, Nos.69012 to 69015 were transferred permanently from the Eastern to the Scottish Region. All were then in the Darlington style with 10in. numbers on the tank side. Ipswich.

69018 cont./
SHEDS:
Sunderland.
West Auckland 31/8/52.
Darlington 1/1/61.

CONDEMNED: 8/10/62.
Into Dar. for cut up 13/11/62.

69019

Darlington 2100.

To traffic 21/1/50.

REPAIRS:
Ghd. 27/10—15/11/52.**L/I**.
Ghd. 2—5/2/53.**N/C**.
Ghd. 29/2—27/3/56.**G**.
Dar. 31/8—12/10/60.**G**.

BOILERS:
 4040.
 4040 reno.25657 15/11/52.
25655 *(exJ71 68278)* 27/3/56.
25724 *(ex68736)* 12/10/60.

SHEDS:
Middlesbrough.
Thornaby 1/6/59.
West Hartlepool 25/3/62.

CONDEMNED: 9/12/63.
Sold for scrap to G.Cohen &
Sons, Cargo Fleet, 8/64.

69020

Darlington 2101.

To traffic 27/1/50.

REPAIRS:
Ghd. 3—24/11/52.**L/I**.
Dar. 6—23/12/55.**G**.
Dar. 1—24/10/59.**G**.

BOILERS:
 4043.
 4043 reno.25659 24/11/52.
25705 *(ex68678)* 23/12/55.
25697 *(ex69021)* 24/10/59.

SHEDS:
York.
Hull Dairycoates 21/2/60.
Darlington 7/10/62.

CONDEMNED: 28/12/63.
Sold for scrap to T. J.Thompson.
Stockton-on-Tees, 12/64.

69021

Darlington 2149.

To traffic 11/4/51.

REPAIRS:
Ghd. 9/11—4/12/53.**H/I**.
Ghd. 8—13/1/54.**N/C**.
Ghd. 13/8—7/9/56.**G**.
Dar. 27/2—26/3/59.**G**.

BOILERS:
25581.
25697 *(ex69024)* 7/9/56.
25551 *(ex68723)* 26/3/59.

SHEDS:
Darlington.
West Hartlepool 13/8/61.

CONDEMNED: 30/9/63.
Into Dar. for cut up 10/10/63.

69022

Darlington 2150.

To traffic 14/4/51.

REPAIRS:
Ghd. 15/9—3/10/53.**L/I**.
Ghd. 3—25/4/56.**G**.
Dar. 20/2—19/3/59.**G**.
Dar. 6—20/10/61.**C/L**.

BOILERS:
25699.
25657 *(ex69019)* 25/4/56.
25693 *(ex68712)* 19/3/59.

SHEDS:
Darlington.
West Hartlepool 10/9/61.

CONDEMNED: 31/12/62.
Into Dar. for cut up 21/5/63.

69023

Darlington 2151.

To traffic 17/4/51.

REPAIRS:
Ghd. 16/11—4/12/53.**L/I**.
Ghd. 13—31/8/56.**G**.
Dar. 20/11—24/12/60.**G**.

BOILERS:
25582.
25739 *(new)* 31/8/56.
25741 *(ex68679)* 24/12/60.

SHEDS:
Blaydon.
Gateshead 7/10/62.
North Blyth 26/10/64.

RENUMBERED:
DEPT'L 59 26/10/64.

CONDEMNED: 18/9/66.
Sold for preservation. 9/66.

69024

Darlington 2152.

To traffic 21/4/51.

REPAIRS:
Ghd. 20/10—7/11/53.**L/I**.
Ghd. 26/6—3/8/56.**G**.
Dar. 21/12/59—1/2/60.**G**.

BOILERS:
25697.
25672 *(ex69010)* 3/8/56.
25736 *(ex68741)* 1/2/60.

SHEDS:
Blaydon.
Heaton 1/10/61.
Gateshead 16/6/63.

CONDEMNED: 23/9/63.
Into Dar. for cut up 3/1/64.

69025

Darlington 2153.

To traffic 26/4/51.

REPAIRS:
Ghd. 3—21/11/53.**L/I**.
Ghd. 16/4—4/5/56.**G**.
Dar. 7/1—8/2/60.**G**.

BOILERS:
25696.
25596 *(ex68674)* 4/5/56.
25672 *(ex69024)* 8/2/60.

SHEDS:
Blaydon.
Tyne Dock 1/10/61.
Gateshead 25/3/62.

CONDEMNED: 28/12/63.
Sold for scrap to T.J.Thompson,
Stockton-on-Tees, 12/64.

69026
Darlington 2154.

To traffic 2/5/51.

REPAIRS:
Ghd. 10—27/2/54.**L/I**.
Ghd. 24/9—12/10/56.**G**.

BOILERS:
25583.
25581 *(ex69021)* 12/10/56.

SHEDS:
Blaydon.
Hexham 6/5/51.
Blaydon 2/11/52.
Heaton 1/10/61.

CONDEMNED: 30/4/62.
Into Dar. for cut up 22/6/62.

69027

Darlington 2155.

To traffic 8/5/51.

REPAIRS:
Ghd. 10—28/8/53.**L/I**.
Ghd. 22/5—15/6/56.**G**.

BOILERS:
25694.
25614 *(exJ71 68272)* 15/6/56.

SHEDS:
Heaton.
Gateshead 25/1/59.

CONDEMNED: 22/10/62.
Into Dar. for cut up 4/4/63.

69028

Darlington 2156.

To traffic 12/5/51.

REPAIRS:
Ghd. 28/9—17/10/53.**L/I**.
Ghd. 24/5—22/6/56.**G**.
Dar. 15/8—8/9/61.**G**.

BOILERS:
25695.
25694 *(ex69027)* 22/6/56.
25739 *(ex69023)* 8/9/61.

SHEDS:
Heaton.
Gateshead 16/6/63.

CONDEMNED: 26/10/64.
Sold for scrap to T.J.Thompson,
Stockton-on-Tees, 12/64.

All four had a General repair at Inverurie: Nos.69012 (15th January 1954), 69013 (25th May 1956), 69014 (30th December 1955) and 69015 (26th August 1954), at which they got 12in. numbers painted on the bunker. Although not withdrawn until 21st February 1961 to 19th February 1962, none got the 1957 BR crest.

Of these four, only No.69014 was fitted with the shunter's step and handrail which caused the figures to be at a slightly higher level than on the others.

On 6th May 1960 Newcastle pilot No.68723 was ex Darlington in original North Eastern Railway green lined livery but with its BR number in its usual place. It also carried the large NER armorial and the BR crest.

A panel of lining was put on the back of the bunker and the only incongruity was the electrification warning signs on bunker and boiler barrel. Newcastle (Central).

Ex works 21st May 1960, York pilot No.68736 had been given the same special treatment. It worked at York until 16th July 1961 when it went to Gateshead shed to work at Newcastle (Central) station. Unlike No.68723, it managed to avoid having the electrification warning flashes put on.

At the end of 1963 only four J72's remained, Nos.69005, 69016, 69023 and 69028 and at their final repair they got the BR crest and 12in. instead of 10in. figures. Gateshead, July 1963.

As these final repairs took place from late 1960 onwards, 69005 (31st January 1962), 69016 (27th January 1962), 69023 (24th December 1960) and 69028 (8th September 1961) they all got the BR crest in its correct heraldic style with lion facing to the left on both sides. Gateshead, July 1963.

Nos.69016 and 69028 were withdrawn in October 1964, but the other two, on 26th October 1964, became Departmental No.58 and No.59. Smokebox plates 69005 and 69023 were taken off and 58 and 59 simply took the place of blacked-out numbers. Gateshead, May 1965.

No.58 was withdrawn on 7th October 1967 and sold for cutting up on 10th January 1968, which made J72 class extinct. No.59 was withdrawn on 18th September 1966 and sold for preservation in working order. It went to the Keighley & Worth Valley Railway and the name JOEM was derived from the names of the owner's parents.

The new owner restored the 69023 number and had it repainted in NER green lined livery, the name then being carried by cast plates. Layerthorpe, May 1977.

J71 CLASS Numerical Index

Original Nos. with 1946 Nos:

No.	1946 No.	Page.
27	—	8
50	8254	20
54	8261	21
70	8235	8
77	8270	25
84	—	16
103	8262	21
137	8298	38
144	—	5
161	8271	25
165	8230	5
168	8236	8
176	8263	21
177	8264	21
179	8265	24
181	8266	24
221	8247	16
224	8248	16
225	—	16
237	8286	32
239	8253	19
240	8287	32
241	8255	20
242	—	11
244	8256	20
248	8267	24
252	8272	25
254	8257	20
260	8258	20
261	8232	5
263	—	8
268	—	12
272	8237	8
275	8241	12
278	—	11
280	8273	26
285	—	12
286	8242	12
296	—	20
299	8231	5
301	8274	26
304	—	5
317	—	5
326	8233	8
338	8259	21
347	8238	11
399	—	5
400	8260	21
401	—	29
402	—	33
403	8243	12
447	—	26
448	—	26
449	8275	26
450	8276	26
451	—	26
452	8277	26
453	—	19
478	—	24
482	8268	24
492	8249	19
493	—	11
494	8239	11
495	8250	19
496	—	19
499	8240	11
501	8251	19
533	8234	8
541	8244	12
572	8278	29
577	8279	29
584	—	12
802	8269	24
811	—	11
969	—	37
972	8297	37
977	8299	38
978	8300	38
980	8301	38
1083	8252	19
1084	8288	33
1085	8280	29
1095	8289	33
1103	8281	29
1123	8245	16
1134	8310	42
1140	8282	29
1142	8283	32
1143	8290	33
1144	—	33
1151	8291	33
1153	8284	32
1155	8292	33
1157	8285	32
1163	—	16
1167	8246	16
1196	8293	37
1197	8294	37
1198	8295	37
1199	8296	37
1314	—	37
1666	—	38
1688	8312	42
1689	8313	45
1690	8314	45
1735	8302	38
1758	—	42
1789	8311	42
1796	8303	41
1797	8304	41
1831	8305	41
1832	8306	41
1833	8307	41
1834	8308	41
1835	—	42
1836	8309	42
1861	8315	45
1862	—	45
1863	—	45
1864	8316	45

1946 & Original Numbers:

1946	Original
8230	165
8231	299
8232	261
8233	326
8234	533
8235	70
8236	168
8237	272
8238	347
8239	494
8240	499
8241	275
8242	286
8243	403
8244	541
8245	1123
8246	1167
8247	221
8248	224
8249	492
8250	495
8251	501
8252	1083
8253	239
8254	50
8255	241
8256	244
8257	254
8258	260
8259	338
8260	400
8261	54
8262	103
8263	176
8264	177
8265	179
8266	181
8267	248
8268	482
8269	802
8270	77
8271	161
8272	252
8273	280
8274	301
8275	449
8276	450
8277	452
8278	572
8279	577
8280	1085
8281	1103
8282	1140
8283	1142
8284	1153
8285	1157
8286	237
8287	240
8288	1084
8289	1095
8290	1143
8291	1151
8292	1155
8293	1196
8294	1197
8295	1198
8296	1199
8297	972
8298	137
8299	977
8300	978
8301	980
8302	1735
8303	1796
8304	1797
8305	1831
8306	1832
8307	1833
8308	1834
8309	1836
8310	1134
8311	1789
8312	1688
8313	1689
8314	1690
8315	1861
8316	1864